Advance Praise for Dead Rita's Wisdom

"Reading *Dead Rita's Wisdom* is like being embraced by a warm, much-needed hug, after a long, emotionally exhausting day. You know the experience will eventually end, so you savor every moment, inhaling the scents, nuzzling against the neck, resting your head against a strong shoulder, exhaling. And then it's over and you're left with a longing, but a realization that you are much more at peace and so, so grateful for having had the experience. Reading the book, I laughed out loud, I cheered, I teared-up. The wisdom resonated so deeply and I can clearly see how intensely the love for your mother ran in your veins. I am so grateful for having shared this experience. Thank you for this gift you have given the world!"

—S. Renee Mitchell, Writer, Speaker, Advocate, Creative Visionary,
Ida B. Wells Award Winner and Pulitzer Prize Nominee 2005/2008

"Rarely does a piece of work come along that stands the potential to provide as much impact as *Dead Rita's Wisdom*. The lessons to be learned are sometimes quirky, elicit a wide range of emotions, are thought provoking and ultimately time tested. Vicky Trabosh has shared her very special relationship with Rita from the heart and in a way that makes you feel as if you were sitting right there with them as it took place. I whole-heartedly recommend you snuggle up and take in everything this book has to offer!"

—Scott Schilling, Speaker, Trainer and
Author of Talking With Giants!

"Victoria Trabosh's book, *Dead Rita's Wisdom*, is written with warmth, humor and an occasional jab to the gut. Your own mother's voice will echo in your head as you digest the profound insights Vicky shares about Rita. Rita reminds me a great deal of my mother, Ruth; she loved her daughter passionately and without question. Although the book could be a quick read, the reader should pause for thoughtf'

—Judith A. McGee,
house Personal Investment Guide

"*Dead Rita's Wisdom* is one of those books that was meant to be written. When Vicky came into my life as a friend, she brought the special spice and spark that makes a friendship rich. I soon discovered that much of that spice came from her mother. For years I have enjoyed the spice of "Dead Rita's Wisdom" as Vicky would insert it into an ordinary life moment and suddenly that moment had added depth.

When Vicky first mentioned the idea of writing this book and naming it *Dead Rita's Wisdom*, I became one of her cheerleaders. I knew others would benefit greatly from the life lessons that Vicky gleaned from her mother and I was right. This book carries more than just wisdom, it stirs your heart as the reader is allowed to brush against the mother-daughter relationship. It allows you to see the richness of relationship and character found in the midst of an imperfect life. It causes the reader to see the treasures that adorn the hardships of life."

—*Janice Seney, Speaker, Artist, Author of* The Heartbeat of God

---

"I can't put it down…love it! Thank you Vicky for bringing to light stories so touching and authentic. Your book is a gift to everyone with a mother who wants to remember their own pearls of wisdom to store in the treasure chest of their soul. *Dead Rita's Wisdom* is a true gift to anyone who wants to discover the pearls of wisdom in their own relationship with their mother…remembering that it was all perfect as it was. This book will touch you at your core. Vicky's stories will awaken in your own memory, the pearls of wisdom gifted by your mother that have made you who you are today. Thank you for creating this wonderful gift which has giving me so much gratitude for all that my mother went through in her life. *Dead Rita's Wisdom* is helping me see the true gift she really was to me!"

—*Katana Abbott, Founder and Co-host* Smart Women Talk Radio, *Contributing Author to* Thank God I, Book 2 *and* Stepping Stones to Success

DEAD *Rita's* WISDOM

Simple words
to help you live
an extraordinary life

V<small>ICTORIA</small> T<small>RABOSH</small>

Wisdom Beneath My Wings Publishing

DEAD RITA'S WISDOM
Simple Words to Help You Live an Extraordinary Life
Victoria Trabosh

ISBN 978-098310089-8
Printed in the United States of America

This book is a work of non-fiction. It is an honest and accurate account of stories of my life, and my mother's, insofar as I have been able to remember and research.

Cover Design by Peter Butler of Urban Creatives PDX
Book Design by Barbara Denney
Publishing Consultant: On the Mark Publishing

Wisdom Beneath My Wings Publishing
2187 SW Main, Suite 201
Portland, Oregon 97205
Visit our website at www.WisdomBeneathMyWings.com

Dedicated to Rita Mae Clark Hoering

Acknowledgements

WRITING A BOOK IS AKIN to a mouse giving birth to an elephant…at least for a person like me. Until now, I hadn't seen myself as a writer. It's waaaay harder than I imagined! And yet, this book is done!

It is humbling to believe that I have a message. And yet, it's through the faith of my mother, and all those who, in big and small ways, believed in me, that this book has taken flight.

To each of you listed here, please accept my love, thanks and gratitude. Without you, *Dead Rita's Wisdom* would not be a reality.

To my dream team, Marcia Wieder, Gonzolo Flores, Tom Flynn, Brad Stauffer, Katana Abbott, Alicia Kent, Harmony Harrison, Andrew Brewer, Kim Boyden and Patti Keating: I learned from each of you to keep working on my dream of bringing this book into existence in spite of my doubts and fears. (Imagine what is possible when we allow others a glimpse into our dreams!)

To my editors, Tamela Viglione, Karla Smith, Harmony Harrison and Diane Hill: Really?! It took four of you!? Indeed! Thank you all for not trying to teach me a verb from a noun…you made this book flow better and allowed my voice to remain. Dead "editor" Rita would have been impressed with each of you!

Margie Kallenback: Thank you for your love and wisdom in my life. How blessed am I to love you. Linda K. Smith: Mom loved you because you are an incredible woman and friend, and Mom had it right! Thanks for so many years of friendship. Julie Sklare: You were there through the very end with Mom…you supported me and gave me comfort and I will always be grateful for you and our friendship. Timothy Newth: You have cried and laughed with me more than any other human being on this earth about Dead Rita – and you never even met her! I love you dearly. Josh Hoering: May Mom's words continue to give you wings and allow you to take your art to the world. You always believed in this project and that support and the story of Mom's words to you in this book were another sign that the book must be written.

Rita Ngarambe: I will forever be indebted to you for asking me to come to Rwanda. It was your name, Rita, that caught my attention. It was your kindness and love that has held our friendship. Of course, Rita would take me to Rwanda! And because of you a portion of the proceeds of this book will flow through to the Itafari Foundation. Never doubt your influence in the world, or on my heart.

Jeff and Dan, beloved brothers: How thankful I am to have you both in my life and to receive your blessing on this book. Mom and I had many hours of conversations about her fierce love and hopes for you both. How I wish she were here to see what incredible men you have both continued to be.

Todd, Tim and Ty: How you got saddled with me as your step-mother, is something I doubt you'll ever recover from. From the beginning, you have shown me more love and grace than I could have ever dreamed of receiving. You are my stepsons in the eyes of the world but you are my sons in the deepest part of my heart.

Tara: Who am I to be so graced to be loved by you? Your love from the beginning smashed all stereotypes of daughters resentful of their fathers who chose a younger bride. But not you! In every sense of the word, you are my daughter. We share a bond so similar to my bond with Mom. She was always sad I never had children of my own. But how wrong she was! Your support, your confidence in this project and your love and friendship with Mom all were part of this perfect plan. My unending love will be with you always.

John my beloved: Little did we know what we would accomplish together. But I knew you were the one, though I had no idea of the depth and breadth of your love. You have sheltered me, supported me, believed in me and laughed at all my jokes. The level of your care and support of my parents, especially Mom, is the least known public part of this journey. And then, when the idea of this book dropped into my brain, you were the first to say, "You have to write this book" after I showed you the first chapter. It was your confidence that made me know I had something to say. It is your strength that gives me courage. And it is your love that has allowed me to accomplish the extraordinary.

To anyone I've overlooked, please accept my apologies. To everyone who said, "When is *Dead Rita's Wisdom* coming out?" or "Couldn't you change the name of the book?" the answers were always "soon" and "no." Thank you for accepting those answers and always believing in me, and the wisdom of Dead Rita.

Love, Vicky

Table of Contents

Communication

Perseverance

Letter to the Children of Rwanda

Muraho. Amakuru? Nitwa Vicky.

I am an orphan.

Losing one's parents is a loss like no other. This book is about my mother, whose wisdom has changed and sustained me long after her death in 1998. For so many of you who have lost a parent through disease, HIV, and the 1994 genocide, this book is a reminder that your loss does not need to be forgotten. That your loss and sacrifice are not in vain.

I am giving a portion of the proceeds of this book to the Itafari Foundation. Working in Rwanda is a privilege I never imagined.

In 2004, I met a woman named Rita Ngarambe, who came to my hometown of Portland to speak for World Vision International about Rwanda's microfinance program. Rita had my attention because of her name—Rita is also my mother's name. Now, Rita Ngarambe holds my friendship and heart because of the quality of her character and her immeasurable love for others.

When we met, we spoke of hope. She told me many of her clients had lost hope. I shared my belief that we are all here to do something—that God wants us to do whatever we can while we are here on earth. She asked me to come to her country and speak about hope.

In June 2005, I came to Rwanda with World Vision. I left your country ten days later hoping I could do more. The Itafari Foundation is about that hope. Itafari (as you know) means brick. And a brick represents the weight of a malnourished child that cannot be comforted. It is the burden that a woman carries down a path as she struggles to find a way to feed her family. And it was the color of the soil that a woman saw as she was being violated face down in the dirt during the genocide. But a brick, an itafari, also represents hope. It is itafari by itafari by itafari that the Itafari Foundation will help strengthen, rebuild, and support the people of Rwanda.

May this book bring you comfort. May this book remind you of the wisdom you received from someone you love, or have loved and lost. And may this book remind you of the wisdom that lies within you—and encourage you to share who you are with those around you.

Getting this book completed only happened when I realized that I could do more for the Itafari Foundation financially by publishing it. Nothing inspires me more than Rwanda. Nothing reminds me more clearly that we honor those who have died more by our action than our grief. Nothing is more important than remembering loss and growing from it.

I am so sorry for your loss. May you honor those you have lost more by your action than your grief. And know you are not forgotten, nor are those you have lost.

Sincerely,
Vicky

"There is sacredness in tears. They are not the mark of weakness, but of power. They speak more eloquently than ten thousand tongues. They are messengers of overwhelming grief ... and unspeakable love."

— *Washington Irving*
(1783 – 1859)

Introduction

WHAT SUSTAINS US? WHAT VOICE reassures us we are capable of accomplishing the impossible? What messages have we received that we will remember all of our lives?

For me, it has often been the great yet simple wisdom of my mother, Rita Clark Hoering. Her love was a guiding force in my life until she died in my arms on October 3, 1998.

She was sixty-five years old and, by my estimation, died twenty years too soon. You see, there was one thing I had always known for certain: That my mother and I would grow old together. That I would care for her when she needed me. That we would be together for a very long time.

Some desires are for material or selfish things. But my intention was noble. This was about love. But growing old together was not meant to be. And yet I was so sure it should have been the way I saw it!

But Rita would have said, "You're wrong, Vic!" In the moment that she died, I realized one of the greatest lessons of my life: that I don't know anything.

Her death took time. Breast cancer first struck in 1996. She recovered, and then, in July 1997, was diagnosed with lung cancer.

Sixteen months, all told—the most heartbreaking and beautiful period of my life with my mother. While it was difficult to watch her body fade, her spirit remained gloriously intact. And our time together was magical—the best and the saddest of times. We were never as present with one another as in those final days.

It wasn't until the moments after her death that I realized my best friend was gone forever.

But her loving wisdom remained. She passed it on to me throughout the years of our time together in word and in action, and the wisdom lives on. I've shared much of it over the years with friends and strangers who have been cheered, comforted, and encouraged. In passing on that legacy, I've been comforted and strengthened as well.

As you might imagine, after my mother passed, she was often

on my mind—and her wisdom was often on my lips. I'd find ways to bring any conversation around to her. My husband John, who'd lived through so much of it at my side, would patiently allow me to go on.

In time, though, he began to call me on it. I'd bring up something about Mom when talking with a stranger, and eventually I'd mention she had died. John would look at me quizzically, with great love and humor, and exclaim, "Your mother's dead?!"

To which I'd respond, with equal humor, "You didn't know?"

So—with tremendous affection and love—I began to refer to her as "Dead Rita." This woman who was dearest mother, greatest friend, most trusted confidante, partner in crime, shopping buddy, role model—and so much more.

She'd have loved it. That's the kind of woman she was. And it was the kind of humor we often shared, especially in those final months together.

Of course, I miss her. But what sustains me, and what has helped and healed others over the years, is what I've often called "Dead Rita's Wisdom."

Dead Rita's Wisdom has been heard over the ages, through many voices. Yet, because Rita herself was unique, as we all are, her wisdom was her own. Rita's words can support, heal, and encourage you, as all true wisdom does.

This book isn't about women or mothers. It's about the people in our lives who support us and sustain us. Throughout this book you'll come to recognize the wisdom and insights shared by those in your own life, living or dead. And when you do, you'll likely hear them in the voice of the person from whom you learned them. Not only can you be taught by these moments, you can be comforted to remember the one who had the kindness and heart to share them.

My life is rich and full. I lack for nothing of importance. But I miss Rita in such a way... Sometimes, when I see older mothers and daughters together, I wonder why I'll never have that chance, the opportunity to be with her here, for a longer time on earth.

And then a little of her wisdom comes to mind: I would never trade the kind of love I experienced even if I could have avoided the level of loss I've felt.

Not all mothers are like Dead Rita. Rita didn't have a mother like Rita! But she lives on in this unabashed tribute. When I think of the words in this book, I hear her voice.

Mom, I dedicate this book to you.

Adversity

Purple Lips Is Here

Dead Rita's Wisdom:
Our greatest burdens can
become our greatest teachers.
There are moments that
change us forever.

HEN I WAS BORN IN 1957, I was a dream realized for my mother. She had always wanted a little girl. After the birth of my older brother Jeff thirteen months earlier, the doctor told her never to have another child because it would most likely result in her death, or the death of the baby. But I was born, I survived, and this was beyond her wildest dreams.

Then they handed me to her. And she saw the port wine stain that started below my nose, covered my mouth and chin, and swathed my neck.

She was devastated for me. She knew how cruel the world would be.

Mom later told me that people would stop to admire me, then see this birthmark, back up a bit, and ask what was wrong. She would patiently explain, and then they'd try to help by responding, "Well, she can wear lipstick."

But Rita knew it wouldn't be that easy.

When I was six weeks old, the doctor burned off the birthmark with dry ice—with no anesthetic. Mom told me that four people held me down. Dry ice was applied directly to my small face to burn off a great portion of the mark. After weeks of blistering and bleeding, it healed. But my lips remained purple, with a scar under my lower lip.

Rita was a great storyteller. I was about four years old when she told me that story, with enthusiasm. Later, when people inevitably asked, "Why are your lips purple?" I could reply with a ready response and without embarrassment. It worked out well.

Until I hit junior high.

Is there some way to stop the cruelty of others towards the weakest of lambs? I was new to this school. We had just moved, and I was naïve about how unkind kids could be.

I was smart. I was on the higher-level track for my grade. I traveled to the same classes with the same kids throughout the day. But somehow, I got on the wrong side of one girl. She was a ringleader—smart and sarcastic. One day, she turned her gaze on me, a pudgy prepubescent twelve-year-old, and she cruelly bestowed upon me the nickname "Purple Lips."

The other kids followed her lead, just as kids do when they're intimidated by a bully. They all chimed in, taunting me with the name *Purple Lips.*

School became torture. I was ridiculed and humiliated, always out of earshot of any teacher who might come to my rescue.

> # What doesn't kill us makes us funnier.
>
> — *Marian Keyes*

Like many bullied children, I endured deep shame and heartache in silence. It got worse and worse. My outgoing, sunny personality turned dim. I began to suffer stomach aches and asked to stay home.

When my mom asked what was going on, I told her. It was Rita's worst fear—that my birthmark would be a burden. And I was a little young yet for lipstick.

She sat me down. "Vicky," she said, "here's what I want you to do. I want you to walk into the classroom, stand up at the front, and say '*Purple Lips* is Here!' If they make a cruel joke about you—laugh! Then make another joke about yourself. And soon they'll see how mean they're being and they'll stop. Don't make fun of them, just yourself. They can't keep hurting you if you pretend it doesn't hurt."

It sounded like a plan. So the very next day, trembling with fear, I walked into the class that brought me the greatest torture and torment: Developmental and Speed Reading. The pit of hell, an image undimmed even now from my adult's perspective.

The bell had not yet rung, and the jackals waited, licking their lips, eager for the chance to pounce. Instead of slinking to my seat, I headed to the front of the room. And I announced in a strong voice, *"PURPLE LIPS* IS HERE!"

The taunting began. They made cruel remarks. They laughed at me.

I laughed at me. I came back with derisive and sarcastic remarks about myself.

Then something shifted. I saw uneasiness in the eyes of the mob. The ringleader seemed unimpressed, but something had changed.

I kept this up day after day, standing at the front of the classroom, taking their cruelty and laughing at myself. It was excruciating, but exhilaration began to blossom inside me. I don't remember how long it took, but I eventually turned every single person around and became friends with them all—even the "evil ringleader" (though when we received our caps and gowns as seniors, I could still look at her and feel pain). She never apologized.

When I first embarked on my grand experiment, I went home and told Mom what I had done.

She looked at me. "You did that? I never could have done that!"

What? I thought. *You didn't MEAN it?* And I realized, then, that she didn't know how wise she really was.

She had, in truth, meant it. But it also took more courage than she could ever have imagined having herself. How funny is that— and how typical of people who are wise in their vision for others but less so for themselves.

The experience actually played a great part in honing my humor and timing—which to this day is directed at my own dunderheaded-ness, not turned cruelly on others. I will always be sensitive to the child or adult who suffers shame or is ostracized. I know that pain.

My purple lips are with me today (and I do wear lipstick). I actually get complimented on their fullness and color. But I'm also still asked on occasion—boldly and crassly by adults, and curiously by children—"Why are your lips *purple*?" I gently explain and answer their questions.

My lips will always help me remember the early wisdom Dead Rita gave me, and how it changed my life. From this, I learned that our greatest burdens can become our greatest teachers.

And I'm thankful.

Your Own Wisdom:

The Most Important Day in Your Life

Dead Rita's Wisdom:
Are you ready for what
the day can bring?

*P*ERFECTLY TAILORED. ALL THE TIME. That was Dead Rita. Great hair. Great figure. Make-up applied beautifully! She did it without thinking. She *always* looked good. I wanted to look just like her. Petite. Well-groomed. Every hair in place.

When I was young, I was mesmerized by my mother's hair. It was a terrific little Barbie bouffant thing, very stylish during the 1960s and 70s. People thought Rita was a hairdresser. I never saw her go out in public without being done up.

Yet she was almost always exhausted. She worked full-time, had the majority of the child-raising responsibilities, kept a spotlessly clean home, cooked like a maniac, and dedicated her entire life to our family. One of her expressions was, "Tired, tired, tired."

"Tired" was an understatement.

As I became a teenager, I began to share the bathroom with her in the morning. In that tiny four-by-five-foot space, her cigarette filled the air with a healthy dose of secondhand smoke, her coffee cooled on the counter, and we'd comfortably start our day together.

I'd glance over at my dear mother. Her eyes would be puffy from a poor night's sleep, she'd be too tired to move, and still she'd be carefully applying her makeup, fixing the hair, then off she'd trot to her bedroom to slip on some lovely dress-for-success outfit—size four—and a spritz of Estée Lauder, and then away to work she'd go.

Captivating—but at what price?

One day I said, "Mom, why do you do this every day when you're so tired?"

She looked at me very seriously. "Vic," she said, "this could be the most important day of my life, and I have to be ready."

Quite a concept for a sixteen-year-old.

Rita's wisdom stuck.

Caring for herself was never about vanity or looking for compliments. She didn't do it for my dad, certainly not for other men, nor for friends. She did it for herself. She did it so she'd be ready to face the day, whatever it may hold. Wanting to emulate Rita in any way I could, I adopted that philosophy.

I was a "big girl." It would have been so easy to believe that, because I was overweight, there was little use in taking care with my appearance. I saw it in other girls—both overweight and "normal"—at school. Some were sloppy and looked worse than they might have.

I, on the other hand, always looked my best.

Dead Rita's words burn bright in me to this day. Her wisdom continues to serve me well. I notice that when I'm "ready," I don't need to think about my appearance for the rest of the day. It takes away any distraction I might have if I were conscious of my look or my attitude.

Now, admittedly, at 50 years old and beyond, there are more times I go out without makeup. Dead Rita would be stunned. But it's a conscious choice, so there are no consequences. I carry my confidence within me.

Dead Rita's wisdom wasn't ultimately about clothes or makeup. It was about being mentally ready for the most important day of your life. Taking care of her physical appearance did this for Rita, more than anything else.

Are you ready for what the day can bring? Are you ready for the most important day of your life? If you're presented with an opportunity, a friendship, the love of your life, will you be ready?

To get ready, resolve to be ready. It's that straightforward and simple.

My husband John took Dale Carnegie classes years ago to learn public speaking. He talked about the "ready chair" in the back of the room. The next speaker on deck sits in that chair and gets ready to speak, preparing himself or herself to run to the front of the room for wild applause and to deliver a successful and inspirational speech.

John told me how he would get ready. He'd center himself. Focus. Aim to inspire. That kind of preparation leads to success.

That's what Dead Rita's ritual was about every day. She even faced her darkest days of cancer that way. When she was too weak to do the simplest of things for herself, I honored her by doing them for her, carrying on the loving ritual. The touch of lipstick. The spritz of perfume. The perfect hair. When others came to visit, she was at peace because she was as ready as she could be.

What a powerful lesson. Be ready. Emotionally. Mentally. Physically. Spiritually. Intellectually. Because it could be the most important day of your life.

And wear good underwear in case you're in a car accident.

Your Own Wisdom:

Weak Ankles

Dead Rita's Wisdom:
The stories we tell ourselves
become our truth.

I DON'T KNOW IF I FELL A LOT when I was young, or if I just wasn't that quick on my feet. But I remember being cautioned not to try certain things because, as Rita said, I had "weak ankles." Rita was afraid I would get hurt, and treated me differently than she treated my brother. She was more protective simply because I was a girl

So I never ice skated, even though Rita had given me skates for Christmas one year. When my Girl Scout troop went roller skating, I was scared to death that I wouldn't be able to do it. When I could, I figured it was only because the laces at the ankle held me up.

I never feared walking in high heels, and I never fell off them. I ran well enough. But I did hurt my ankle after I jumped up to grab a leaf off a tree and landed in a slight hollow in the ground. How could landing in a shallow hole have caused this kind of injury? Clearly I had weak ankles.

Thank God my ankles were not necessary for my career, marriage, friendships, or parenthood. But they were definitely a limiting trait I believed about myself.

When I married John, one of the sports he and his family all enjoyed was downhill skiing. No problem. I figured I would be the cook, making the best deli sandwiches they'd ever had for their mid-day lodge breaks.

When John or the kids would ask me why I wasn't skiing, I'd always reply, "I can't—I have weak ankles."

Then, one day during spring break, I took the kids to Mt. Bachelor to ski. Bringing taxes to work on in the lodge, I decided, would be an idyllic way to keep me content and keep my ankles safe. I'd be perfectly happy just sitting and watching out the huge windows as others skied.

I was mesmerized—not by the taxes, but by the beautiful scene unfolding outside those windows. Sun, snow, people of all sizes, shapes and ages buzzing up and down the hill—falling, laughing, and getting back up. No snow patrol with stretchers removing skiers as they clutched their ankles in agonizing pain.

Too bad I have weak ankles, I thought—almost as if I had a disability.

But I'd caught the bug. Once home, I decided to surprise my family by taking ski lessons—ankles be damned—on an indoor ski training zone. I brought my oldest stepson Todd with me, and we skied on a rolling carpet. Very cool. (I couldn't figure out how to get up once I was down, but there's no wisdom in that—it was just something I conquered later.)

Todd kept my secret. As the family headed out for a week of holiday skiing, I announced to John at the last moment that I was going to try to ski. I looked the part (love those ski fashions!) and off to Mt. Bachelor we went.

After half a day of ski instruction, John and the boys took me to the top of Mt. Bachelor, and down I skied.

It was one of the most exhilarating things I have ever done.

I DON'T HAVE WEAK ANKLES! I thought on the way down— quickly followed by, *I DON'T KNOW HOW TO STOP AND I DON'T TURN VERY WELL!*

As I picked up speed, John raced after me with great concern, and I began to repeat to myself, *"Thank you, Jesus! Thank you, Jesus! Thank you, Jesus! Thank you, Jesus!"*

But I continued straight down the mountain. As the terrain flattened out, it was either stop or ski straight through the lodge and out to the parking lot. So I did what any new skier would have done—I threw myself to the ground instead of attempting to break a land speed record. It was the equivalent of a belly flop in a backyard pool. The snow flew. As I came to a commanding halt and the explosion of snow settled, I looked up to see a 10-year-old boy standing calmly five feet from where I had landed.

"Nice stop," he said, without the slightest hint of a smirk.

Later I called Mom to tell her of my accomplishment.

"How did you do that?" she said. "You have weak ankles!"

There is no question she had believed it all those years—and no question that she had only been trying to keep me safe. But what a limiting belief.

The stories we tell ourselves become our truth. Another's truth for us can also become our reality.

How many things are said to us, how many things do we say to others, and how many things do we say to ourselves that don't help, but truly limit experiences and undermine confidence? Things that are said with absolute certainty—that are completely untrue?

I look at how differently I have treated my grandsons and granddaughters. If I take them to the park and they start swinging on the monkey bars, I encourage and support the boys. But to the girls, I've heard myself say, "Careful. Now be careful. Be careful."

Am I teaching these girls to limit themselves while allowing the boys to experience all they can (possibly including a conk on the head)?

In what areas of your life do you believe you are weak? Is it true? Or is it a story, an anecdote, an insinuation you have heard or repeated for so long that you've never really explored the truth? What messages do you give to others that limit them, instead of expanding their lives?

I'm no writer. I've said that for years, simply because Dead Rita was a great writer and I didn't write the way she did. I don't know a noun from a verb. Because of that, I not only "can't write," I also "can't speak a foreign language." In these areas I have "weak ankle syndrome." But that's a psychosomatic ailment. My ankles are not weak.

I do write. And I speak a bit of the following languages: Italian, Hebrew, Japanese, broken English, and my two favorites—Russian and Kinyarwanda. I do so in spite of the stories within me.

It's important to listen to the stories you're told—and the ones you tell—and decide for yourself if they're truth or fiction. Decide for yourself how they'll affect your journey. That discovery will bring you true wisdom and the confidence to fully take on life.

Your Own Wisdom:

If You're Mad, Get Glad

Dead Rita's Wisdom:
Being angry is a choice.

*T*HE LOVE OF RITA'S LIFE was a man named Lee. He was the older brother of a friend. They met in Norwalk, Ohio, and fell in love. When he joined the Air Force and went off to war, Rita waited for him. She was the perfect girl back home: lovely, sweet, pure, completely committed, and in love.

But when Lee came home once on leave, his mood was strange.

"It's a girl," he said, handing Rita a cigar.

She looked at him, baffled, not at all sure what he was saying.

He went on, telling her that he'd gotten another girl pregnant, and he wouldn't be marrying Rita.

She was crushed and completely blindsided—though her naïveté was perhaps a bit extreme even by 1950s standards. She never really recovered. Then one day, John Hoering walked into the Price Store where she worked. Handsome and older than Rita by eight years, he had relocated from New York City where he'd been born and raised. He stuttered so badly no one could understand him. He was a salesman— and a bullshitter—so no one liked him. But Rita took pity on him.

Something of a scoundrel, my future dad fell deeply for this sweet young thing. Rita's mother hated him, sensing in him, I'm sure, qualities that she herself possessed. But Rita married John Hoering in 1955, deciding that if she couldn't be with Lee, she must marry another.

Though she loved my father, she admitted in later years that her

Parents' wedding. Rita, John, Loretta, 1955

feelings were nothing like what she felt for Lee. And here lies the part my mother played in the cycle of sadness and verbal abuse that was to accelerate over the course of forty-two years of marriage.

The first few years were good. Poor, but good. My father had difficulty holding decent jobs. He was a big dreamer and an even bigger risk taker, and lost everything they had more than once.

He was also a man of great humor—and love. He did love my mother very much, but he loved her badly. Over time he grew angry, especially at Rita. Perhaps he was aware of the ways he didn't meet her expectations. He used words like gunshots, directing them at her over and over and over again. Where her mother had left off, Dad picked up.

Rita tried to ease his anger and bitterness by cajoling him, sacrificing, submitting, surrendering, conceding, and playing the martyr. As the focus of his verbalized anger, she tried to brush it off, but it was hard to ignore.

I was in my teens when she found success in business. She was admired and respected by her peers and friends, and the mixed messages from my father grew tiresome at last. She had discovered a new strength, and she began to shut him out in every way: mentally, physically, emotionally, and financially.

"Well," she would say in response to one of his rants, "if he's mad he'll just have to get glad."

How powerful that was for me. I got along better with my father than anyone, and yet I still feared his anger. Mom's wisdom helped me keep that fear in check—with anyone I encounter today, in fact, who uses anger as a weapon.

Mad? Get glad. You don't accomplish a lot with anger. If you sense that anger is being used as a tool against you, you can choose to make the other person's anger not your problem. Physical and mental abuse should not be tolerated.

My mother stayed with my father until she died. But she was protected from his anger in those final years of her life because the two of them came to live in our home—and because of the choices she began to make not to tolerate his attacks.

Now, if he'd get "out of line," Rita would say, "Do you want me to go get Vicky?"

"No!" he'd reply, and calm down.

It's a sad day when the daughter becomes the referee. But life isn't fair. Feeling safe is more important than making everything appear fine or tolerating another's anger at your own expense.

Dead Rita herself rarely seemed angry, even in the face of her situation. The moment she chose not to be affected—infected, really—by my father's outbursts was a tremendously empowering lesson for us both.

Are you mad? Well you'll just have to get glad. Because who—or what—are you truly angry at anyway? Being angry is a choice. A choice my father made, time and again.

We get upset about the smallest of things. We fly off the handle without thought to the consequences of our actions, especially in the ever-increasing pace of today's world. Got a little road rage? Day didn't go your way? Get over it. If you can't, get some help. See a therapist. Discover the roots of the anger. Then you'll get glad.

Obviously, deep-seated anger that comes from abuse shouldn't be lightly brushed off, nor should any form of anger for which a few words of wisdom don't suffice. I want to be clear about that.

But so much anger in the world is actually laziness. The easy way out. Not owning up to the fact that not all goes well at all times, and that there is no deep conspiracy against you this fine day. It's life. Get a grip. Get glad. You'll find getting glad is a simple antidote to being mad.

Your Own Wisdom:

"I Will Not Be Like My Mother"

Dead Rita's Wisdom:
You can find your greatness
in the face of destruction.

*T*RUTH BE TOLD, MY MOTHER'S childhood was bleak. She was born in Norwalk, Ohio, in 1931 to an unwed, sixteen-year-old named Loretta. The new father, Johnny Clark, was equally unprepared and uninterested. Though they would eventually marry, their union would end in divorce. It was a life of unkindness with bouts of violence that would touch and shape an innocent child.

My grandmother Loretta was beautiful and intelligent and selfish. She was with many men in an era when women couldn't easily get away with such behavior.

Rita told me she learned to dance when Loretta took her along to bars. There Loretta would force little Rita to dance with her until a man would ask Loretta to dance. Then little Rita would sit and watch her mother dance late into the night.

They lived on "the wrong side of the tracks." While still together, Loretta and Johnny engaged in physical fights that made Rita cower in fear. Later, she would beg her mother and whatever man she was living with not to embarrass her in front of her friends. Rita was a good girl. A virgin until the moment she married my father. She felt such shame and so detested her life that she determined, at a very young age, not to become her mother.

Loretta was not an attentive mother. Joining the war effort, she left Rita with her mother, Anna—a godsend, for it was Anna who

Anna (great grandma)   *Loretta (grandma) circa mid-1940s*

provided the unconditional love that Rita so desperately needed and deserved. Anna was a hell-raiser too, and she fought with Loretta. But it was different from the fights between Rita's parents, because the anger was never directed at Rita. Though Anna's life was also tragic, her positive influence on her granddaughter helped protect her from at least some of Loretta's destructive behavior.

It was while she was in her grandmother Anna's home that Rita made the decision—at the age of four—that would change her life and all those who would come to be touched by her. Rita told me the story of watching Loretta through the screen door of Anna's home, laughing and walking arm in arm with her girlfriends down the street, with no apparent care in the world. As Rita watched her mother she told me she made a decision and declared to herself, *"I will not be like my mother."*

Four years old. What pain and heartache must she have already suffered to have given her the focus to know what she would *not* become? Despite all that she endured, and though she remained haunted by a sense of shame and inadequacy all her life, Rita persevered to become an outstanding mother and woman in her own right.

The life she suffered as a child was the reason for much of her goodness. She knew, firsthand, how easily a child's life could be destroyed. Yet she overcame, in spite of her fears, because she wanted more—not only for herself but for the others in her life as well.

I believe she was much more successful in helping others than she was in helping herself. Knowing all I did about her past, I always begged her to get help, to seek counseling. But she refused. She couldn't open up about her pain. In a funny turn of events, she did finally start seeing a counselor a few months before she died—and she loved it. "Vic," she said, "this is great! I love talking with this therapist!"

Frankly, I believe the pivotal point for her was sixty-one years prior to that discovery when, as a four-year-old, she embraced the wisdom that would affect so many: "I will not be like my mother."

Who will you choose not to become? Could that decision be the one that alters your life and the lives of others for years to come? Might the wisdom that you receive in a moment of great pain or clarity serve you in a way for which you will always be thankful?

Nothing should be wasted in life. Not kindness, not glory, not a mistake, and certainly not pain. We can learn from it all. It may take years for goodness to grow out of darkness or pain, but I believe all things can work together for good. While we may not be able to see the future, we can choose behaviors that serve a purpose other than to destroy. If we can find our own greatness in the face of destruction, we win—and pain is the loser.

Your Own Wisdom:

Don't Fight His Battles

Dead Rita's Wisdom:
Stand up. Fight your fight.
Let those you love
do the same.

HEN I WAS ABOUT TWELVE, it was my job to watch my younger brother during the summer. Both parents worked and I was happy to be home with Danny all day, keeping him entertained, fed, and safe. He was six years younger than I, and a great little guy. I was fiercely protective of him and loved him dearly.

There were a lot of young boys in the neighborhood, and Danny would go play, checking in throughout the day. As with most children, he'd have some squabbles. Danny would come home to tell me he'd been wronged—and I'd go charging off to the offending child's house to avenge my brother. He would be thrilled, following along because his big sister would be about to give 'em "what for." I'd then head home, quite upset, with Danny in tow. Hours later, or sometimes only minutes, these same kids would show up to play... and Danny would happily go out the door. With me still a wreck.

When Rita would get home, I'd tell her about it. More often than not, she'd meet my frustration with a laugh. "Don't fight his battles," she'd say. "They're kids and they don't take it as seriously as you do. It's his job to figure it out."

I finally got the message, and I stopped. Even when Danny would come home and ask me to get involved, I'd kick him back out of the house to—yes—fight his own battles.

> It is one of the
> most beautiful
> compensations in
> life that no man
> can sincerely try
> to help another
> without helping
> himself.
>
> — *Ralph Waldo Emerson*

Caring for others at personal cost can be exhausting, ineffective, and unsettling. It's often not appreciated by those being "rescued." Over the years, I've come to believe that excessive "saving" of others is really a response to the need to save something within oneself. In this case, within me.

I certainly believed that I needed to save Rita—from Dad, from her own low self-esteem, from her mother, from her life. I didn't save her. She saved herself. But at the time I was so emotionally invested that it took its toll on me.

When she died in my arms on October 3, 1998, I knew the moment she was gone. She didn't make a sound. But I felt her life leave her body. And at the same time, a huge, unknown weight lifted off of me. It was literally physical. With all the grief I felt, I also realized I no longer needed to protect her. The relief was tangible.

"Rescuer" was never my assigned role in life; I assumed the position. It was a noble cause in my mind. With my mother, the rescuer role I took on was borne from a perceived need to provide for her what she didn't provide for herself: confidence, inner faith in her abilities, and an acknowledgement of who she was.

But I believe that spending too much time fighting another's battles, healing another's hurts, focusing only on the needs of others, may be your own soul saying to you, "What about me?" It's a way of diffusing or avoiding issues much closer to home—issues in your own life where you are perhaps not meeting your full personal potential or standing up to those you should.

No one can or should fight my battles. Not my husband, my friends, my family, or my colleagues. I don't want to be as good—or bad—as another dictates. The world can be a cruel place when you need a compliment, a confirmation, a sign. But internally, your own quiet voice is just waiting to be heard. To express what you know, to fight the battle for yourself.

What you do for others you must also do for yourself. By fighting your own battles, you will give others the courage to do the same. Stand up. Fight your fight. Let those you love do the same. You might be surprised at just how empowering this can be.

Your Own Wisdom:

Honesty

Yes, But…

Dead Rita's Wisdom:
Know yourself well so that
you can accept the truth
of your greatness.

*D*EAD RITA LOVED A GREAT philosophical discussion. The more obscure the position, the more she enjoyed discussing the possibilities. She certainly had opinions, but she loved to look at issues from every angle. She didn't accept a lot on faith (including faith). She wanted to know why—somehow believing the knowing why would help her take a singular position. What I noticed was instead of saying she agreed with a truth about herself, not an easy position to take, she often said, "Yes, but…"

Rita and I began a true friendship when I was about fourteen. She was always my mother, of course. I always respected her and her place in my life. But once I hit my teen years, we would talk for hours. As we shared, I could see in her all of her beauty, her greatness, her potential. It was as if I had on special "truth goggles"—and I never hesitated to tell her what I saw.

When I attempted to show her the person she truly was, rather than the inadequate person she believed herself to be, the conversations became difficult. Our heart-to-hearts were always peppered with, "Yes Vic, that's true, but…"

I hated those words, because I knew my darling mother would not be moved to see the point or accept anything great about herself.

I certainly received the same kind of insight when she looked at me. But the big difference between us was this: I accepted her words as the truth, more often than not. "That makes sense," I'd think—and off I'd go to do as she suggested. From my earliest years on, we talked like this, sharing conversations that were always age-appropriate and chock-full of wisdom.

Though young, I was wise and aware—especially about Rita. She always appreciated my observations. Then she'd throw in a "Yes, but..." She was unable to accept many of the truths I saw in her.

Her resistance came from her insecurity, the years of put-downs, first from my grandmother and then from my father. And here was her daughter—someone who had no thought of undermining her—telling her the truth. Trying to awaken her to all that was good and great about her.

I so wanted her to step into her own greatness. On those occasions that she did, she was fabulous.

I wasn't the only one who saw this unrealized potential—she touched and amazed everyone who knew her. Yet, her low self-image remained stronger than any words of encouragement or praise from a loved one or a stranger. Maybe it's because those she first trusted to love her failed her so badly. When we lack a strong inner foundation due to too little emotional support, perhaps it's also true that while the voice we most heed is our own, it doesn't always tell us the truth. That voice just repeats the lies it has been told.

Our hearts are so fragile. If they're broken or damaged too often, they cannot beat at full strength. I believe this was true of Dead Rita. Her inability to reach her full potential made me angry at times, and I was always frustrated. And after twenty-six years of long conversations that should not have been filled with "Yes, buts," one of my real regrets is that Rita never accepted who she was as seen through the eyes of another who could see her so clearly. There were many conversations that ended with, "I wish I could see the woman you see Vic, but I just can't. I don't know her."

After she died, I received a wonderful gift from my mother. It was, I believe, the last piece of wisdom I ever heard in her voice. It was 2004, and I was at a coaching retreat.

It was a life-changing and very grounding time for me. I had come to some realizations about who I truly was and what I could bring to the world. That knowledge brought peace—not euphoria, but a settling in my soul about who I was.

As I sat journaling on this last day of the retreat, I was filled with serenity. Then, as if Mom was whispering in my ear, I heard her say to me, "Vic, you have learned what I never knew. You have learned who you are, and now no one will have to spend his or her life trying to take care of you the way you cared for me."

And she was gone.

I literally stopped writing, and realized that this is what each of us must do.

We must know ourselves. We must understand ourselves so well that we are never a reflection of what others say—good or bad. We can then be our personal best in our given circumstances. There will be fewer "Yes, buts" when someone tries to tell us who we are and what they believe to be true.

The time and energy wasted, the opportunities lost because of our fears and doubts! Self-reflection isn't always easy—but it doesn't have to take forever. We must strive to find an acceptance of ourselves, our circumstances, our experiences, our hurts, and our joys.

You may be tempted to deflect this wisdom by saying, "Yes, but you don't know what has happened to me." What's happened isn't what's relevant. When you accept that experiences can be learned from, that they need not be wasted, and there is great wisdom in your life, you'll be able to say, "I have learned who I am. And no one will have to spend their life trying to show me what I appear not to see, but what they know is true."

Change your "Yes, but" to "OK—I accept this as true." You'll see a change in your life, and the effect on yourself and others will confirm that the "you" you've come to know and accept is a positive force to be reckoned with!

Your Own Wisdom:

You're Flat

Dead Rita's Wisdom:
Seek out people who tell you
the honest truth, and tell
that truth yourself.

*M*OTHER ALWAYS THOUGHT I WAS wonderful. When I look back, I don't remember being showered with compliments. But when she told me I did something well, it really meant something to me. She may have been insecure about herself, but she was supremely secure about who I was and what I was capable of. Her honesty and support were always about helping me be the best I could be.

She did not, however, think I could sing. That certainly never stopped me! When I was young I adored singing. I've always had a great memory for lyrics—I can hear a song just once or twice and have it memorized. Consequently, I sing to the radio, CDs, TV, commercials, small animals and in my head.

I was always in school choirs and Rita sometimes came to the performances but never had many positive things to say. She played music and had a great ear, and heard every child soprano's screech, every missed lyric. She wasn't just critical of school assemblies. Any musical group or singer was fodder for her criticism, though given without malice. She simply couldn't help but comment on what, to her, was obvious.

One of the highlights of my high school career was my acceptance to All City Choir in Fort Wayne. I was chosen by audition, and was beside myself with excitement as I raced home to share the news with

> ## "I love you, and because I love, I would sooner have you hate me for telling you the truth than adore me for telling you lies."
>
> — *Pietro Arentino*

Mother. Her response was not, perhaps, what I most wanted to hear.

"How did you get into that? You can't sing!"

Yet because she had given me the wisdom to believe in myself and always strive to do my best, sing I did—with enthusiasm! Occasionally she would attend a concert, be critical as expected, and that was that.

As I got older, I joined church choirs. Though my voice was not solo quality, I loved to sing more than I cared about perfection, and I continued to entertain myself.

When Rita was in the last week of her life, she needed constant care, and I was by her side the majority of the time. My daughter-in-law Laura was helping me one day, and Mom was very quiet and still. From the time I was small, Rita and I had sung together all the old songs: *Mairzy Doats, Now is the Time, Down By the Old Mill Stream.* I thought I'd serenade her one more time. I began to softly croon *Down By the Old Mill Stream.* Laura was looking on lovingly, and Rita was lying quietly, her eyes closed. It was a wonderful moment. When I finished, Laura smiled at me, and Mother—who had been perfectly quiet—suddenly said, "You're flat!"

I burst out laughing. Laura was horrified—but I knew Rita was there in spirit and with love. She meant no harm; she certainly didn't mind the singing. This woman, who I couldn't imagine life without, was completely whole in her mind despite the pain and ravages of cancer. For me, her remark made all the other things she'd said to me in those last few months as real and honest as her summation of my song.

When you're "flat" in some part of your life, who tells you? Are you interested in hearing the truth or do you just want to hear the positive? Those we trust the most must also be the most honest with us—who better to give us the kind of information that will allow us to be our personal best?

Seek people in your life who care enough to tell you when you're "flat." Be the kind that others seek when they want truth. And know that with the right to tell another when they're flat also comes the responsibility to tell them when they're incredible. The good news is, nobody's flat all the time—even the most inexperienced of song-birds will occasionally hit a beautiful note. That's the honest truth.

Your Own Wisdom:

Liar

Dead Rita's Wisdom:
Lying just doesn't work.

I LIVED TO HAVE A BARBIE when I was little. I would dream so much about it that I would awake expecting to find her sitting on my dresser, her beautiful blond hair pulled back in a perky ponytail—just as I had seen her in my dreams.

I must have been about four years old when I received the longed-for doll. With her brunette bouffant, however, this Barbie was a great disappointment. She was not the blond beauty I had dreamed of. Still, I never said a word. I knew, even as a child, how tight money was and that this gift was an extravagance.

My mother would make the most exquisite Barbie clothes while I was in school. Coming home, I would find a tiny coat complete with a little fur collar and buttons. A perfectly sized dress. The details were amazing—one of the many art forms Rita created. But it wasn't enough for me. So I concocted a story for the neighbor girl. I told her that a Ken doll lived on top of our refrigerator.

My little neighbor and I would solemnly gaze up at the refrigerator and I would say with a mixture of awe and reverence, "Yep. Right up there. Nope. Can't bring him down. Too precious."

I began, in fact, to lie about everything. I was expressive. The bigger the lie, the better. The lies got out of control, until finally one day I told Rita a whopper. I don't even recall now what it was. But out it came, with a totally straight face and no shame.

She looked at me quietly and said, "Vicky, you're lying. I don't believe you. And furthermore, I'm not going to believe anything you say again."

There was no question in my mind that Rita meant it, because she didn't say things she didn't mean. I was stunned.

Soon after, when I shared something completely truthful with her, she'd say, "You're lying."

I realized that she was serious about stopping my impulse to lie. I don't know how I understood, at such a young age, the lesson she was teaching, but from that moment I turned into a fierce truth teller. Each time Rita would say I was lying when I was telling the truth, I'd regroup and understand she was looking for consistency. And I just kept telling the truth. Over and over and over again.

After a time, Rita began to trust me again. Her trust was so important to me. I started to tell her the truth even when she didn't want to hear it! If I did happen to lie, her fabricator meter would flutter, she would look at me and simply say, "Liar."

It felt like a scene from a movie—like I'd suddenly been caught in the glare of a sweeping searchlight while inching along a prison wall. It was impossible to escape the bright beam of that one accusatory word.

I valued my mother's love and respect so much. I realized that telling her the truth was more important than any stories I might have an impulse to tell. I went, then, in the other direction. I became the narc, the snitch, the whistle-blower. It definitely didn't help my relationship with my older brother—his sins were no longer secret. But because I chose to keep nothing from Rita, she advised me wisely and kept me out of typical teenage trouble.

"Are they going to be drinking at the party?" *Yes.* "You can't go."

"Did you drive in your friend's car when I said that you couldn't?" *But Mom, we just wanted to go to McDonald's!* "You're grounded and you're not going out this weekend."

That's how it went. I would tell her, without prompting, what friends were doing. What people were saying. About my concerns for the future. And we would talk. When she'd turn down my request to go to a party because I'd been open about the potential for drinking or drugs, I could then easily tell my friends my mother had said I couldn't go. I know I missed a lot of opportunities to have bad experiences. Then and now, thirty-five years later, I'm so much better for it.

No matter how old I got, if I said something that didn't ring true,

Rita would look at me with a twinkle in her eye and say, "Liar." I'd go back to that time when, as a child, I was so struck because she'd told me she wouldn't believe me anymore.

When does lying serve a person well? Rarely. The truth has its consequences. But lying delays the natural, inevitable outcome of any life story.

Lying and embellishing don't work. My stepchildren know me very well. They know that my stories can, at times, be fantastical. I'm both proud and ashamed to say I learned everything I know about telling a fantastic tale from my dad. But my family calls me on it—literally—by making a noise like a warning beep and then yelling, "Embellishment! Embellishment!"

Embellishing is a form of lying, really. I'm pleased to say I haven't heard that chant regularly for years now. It always takes me back to Dead Rita. She kept me in check, and because of her I've made it part of my value system not to lie. So embellishment is really not an option, either.

The wisdom you've always heard about lying is golden wisdom. It never changes. It's not "case-specific." There is nothing honorable about lying, though facing the consequences of having lied is an opportunity for growth.

Dead Rita's adamant response to lying makes American writer Eric Hoffer's words more powerful for me: "We lie loudest when we lie to ourselves."

To keep faith and trust in ourselves requires the strongest character of all. And through the truth, we truly can be set free.

Your Own Wisdom:

You Should Look as Good Going as You Do Coming

Dead Rita's Wisdom:
Final impressions last forever.

*D*O YOU EVER LOOK AT the back of your head? Do you spend as much time making the back of you look as good as your front? Dead Rita did. She was always checking out her back side—her entire back side.

She was really good at doing her hair. She colored it, permed it, cut it, teased it, and shellacked it. There was rarely a hair out of place by the time she was done. Every morning it was makeup first, then hair. She was meticulous. Once she was done, she'd turn around with a mirror in one hand and a comb in the other, carefully making the back look just as perfect as the front. She'd dress for work, twist around in the mirror, confirm that no panty lines marred her lovely suit, and check for runs in her hose. Then off she'd go—bothering neither to glance at herself in a mirror again nor reapply any more makeup—other than a little lipstick—the rest of the day.

I'd ask her why she'd spend so much time on the back side, and she'd say, "You should look as good going as you do coming. People watch you walk away and everything should be in place."

Guess how many times I do not look at the back of my head after fixing my hair? Her words burn in my ears. As I glance at someone "going" who looked great from the front, but less so from the back (a head of hair that looks like it was caught in an unresolved pillow fight, for example), I think of Rita.

Me, mom, Jeff, circa early 1960s

Dead Rita's wisdom about looking good "going" is really about the bigger issue of how we present ourselves in life. What impression do we leave? First impressions take seconds to form. That's the "front" of us. But final impressions last forever. Often we have the chance to build upon a first impression, change it for the better if need be, and leave a lasting image of ourselves that truly speaks to who we are. That's the "going" part—the back of us.

It's about depth of character, not just surface. Beautiful men and women have a distinct advantage when they walk into a room. Depending on what they say or do, that beauty will deepen, or it'll be a miscue about their true character by the time they say goodbye.

Great intelligence is the same. I've heard people described as wicked smart. I've met wicked smart. I've coached executives who work with wicked smart. Often the wicked smart aren't so smart… just wicked. Greed, aggressive behavior, leadership that lacks vision, and total disregard for those who work as hard as they do but are maybe not as "intelligent"—these are the traits sometimes inherent in wicked smart individuals. This fnal character or impression shows itself for what it is when the person leaves the room. The greatness of the gift of intelligence is lost when not applied to its best and highest use.

When you express unkindness or superiority, your intelligence is never evident. Instead, your fears, doubts, and insecurities are what you leave behind.

Walk into a convenience store. Smile at the clerk (who smiles back). There's your first impression. Now rush to pick up your items, get to the counter, realize you're running late, get impatient, suddenly turn into a jerk, pay, and leave. The clerk who smiled at you now watches you leave his store and says without emotion, "What a @#%!" Guess what final impression you just left.

Life can be a bit of a convenience store experience. We're rushing all the time. Overdoing it. Leaving the wrong impression. Often undoing the great work we wanted to accomplish and, in hindsight, leaving things unfinished and unresolved behind us.

Dead Rita took her time in the morning. She used it not only to get ready physically, but mentally. Her face was on, her game was on. And she rarely slipped.

She's gone, but not forgotten. I know that finding people who knew her would bring up great memories of who she was. When I took her ashes back to Norwalk, Ohio, to bury them in her grandmother's grave, I connected with her old friends from high school, who all described Mother exactly as I saw her. It was amazing. The stories were the same. Her "front" was in the stories she had told me. The "back" of her was confirmed by the memories shared by her high school chums.

Look at your back in a mirror and check out the impression you leave. See if you find it pleasing. If not, take just a bit more time. Slow down long enough to know that you've done what you can to leave a great first impression. And then choose to do nothing that will change another's positive impression of you or your actions.

Your Own Wisdom:

I Don't Trust Her

Dead Rita's Wisdom:
Stop second-guessing yourself
and listen for the truth.

*I*T WAS A JOY FOR me when my parents moved from the Midwest to join us in Oregon in the early 1990s. Our lives were busy and full. But to have Rita with me was the greatest of gifts. We had always been such good friends—best friends—and I'd never found phone calls and letters to be adequate enough while we were apart. I'd wished so often that she were around. That wish was granted when she and my father moved in with us.

I had, at the time, a friend with whom I was close. But it was a friendship that I found myself questioning. I somehow didn't trust this friend; there was something inauthentic about her. Yet I didn't trust myself, either, feeling that I wasn't being generous enough in spirit, that perhaps I was imagining her behavior or intentions. I'm not one to doubt the sincerity of another, and yet I was troubled.

This friend, as it turned out, was not at all pleased when I told her of Rita's impending move to come live with us. Her relationship with her own mother was neither healthy nor happy. She felt that if Rita and I did indeed have the relationship I described, then this new living arrangement would be sure to destroy it. Her doubts did nothing to dissuade me from my excitement or belief that Mother's presence would be a wonderful thing for everyone—including my friend.

Once my parents were settled, I invited my friend over to visit.

> The two words 'information'
> and 'communication' are
> often used interchangeably, but
> they signify different things.
> Information is giving out;
> communication is getting through.
>
> — *Sydney J. Harris*

She and my mother had a very pleasant conversation. It was similar to the one Rita had shared with my boyfriend of old, "fast food ... Jack." After my friend left, I asked Mother what she thought of her.

She knew how much I liked my friend, and how close we were. Yet she said in her typical forthright way, "I don't trust her."

My worst fears were realized. I had never expressed the slightest doubts about this friendship or my friend's motives to my mother or to anyone else. Yet, in my heart of hearts, I didn't trust her and— please hold your cards, we have a bingo—Dead Rita had nailed it.

I hadn't wanted to believe what I feared most: that this was not a healthy relationship. Afterward, I kept trying to make the friendship work, but my heart was not in it. From then on, our friendship quickly faded because I wasn't willing to lie to myself anymore. Getting together was no longer a priority and the relationship ended.

And I lost... nothing. Isn't that the way it is when we remove people from our lives who don't really meet our level of expectation? Some of these relationships can be co-dependent, artificial, hurtful, abusive, expensive, emotionally charged, or dramatic. (Not all at once, I hope!) They truly don't serve the greater good of bringing out the best in us as individuals, or us in them.

All relationships in our lives should be monitored to ensure that the other person is bringing us what we need in our lives, and that we bring them what they need in theirs.

If you don't instinctively trust someone—and you're not diagnosed with a paranoid personality disorder—do not ignore your higher self's message. I think I avoided a lot of mistakes and missteps in my life because my higher voice was Rita's. We shared that kind of communication. I told her everything... much to her dismay at times! But she, in turn, shared her wisdom and maturity on issues that I, as a child, had no perspective on. And I believed her. That was my gift to her, I think, and it brought her great joy as well— to be heard and listened to so closely.

When I got older, I knew wisdom. Though I didn't always listen to myself, I came close, so that when I did stop to pay attention, I was able to say, "I knew that!" The more you say that, the more you'll know that you know. Stop second-guessing yourself and listen for that truth. You will rarely be led wrong. And when you are wrong, you'll know that too!

To understand your instincts, simply quiet your mind, and then trust yourself and the wisdom you have. If you must ask another, as I sometimes do, listen for the confirmation. Listen for the something you may have missed. But most importantly, listen for the wisdom.

Your Own Wisdom:

Whisker Watch

Dead Rita's Wisdom:
Keep your promises, even when
no one else is looking.

*M*ANY WOMEN THROUGH TIME HAVE made a private pact. Often the issue is not discussed in polite circles; never have I heard it spoken of in mixed company. And though it's important, it's a very sensitive issue. The issue is women's whiskers, which begin to grow as we age. They're stubborn little buggers and any women who let them grow unabated are left sporting a "Fu Manchu" type of beard. As we spot them in the mirror or feel them on a previously smooth chin or upper lip, we begin to remove them with great dispatch. But WHAT IF, God forbid, they were left to grow? Not acceptable! So it's important to identify another person, preferably a woman, who will agree with all seriousness to keep our whiskers down in case we're hospitalized or in a coma, or just having a really bad couple of months!

My mother and I had carefully discussed this worrisome issue and I had solemnly agreed to serve as her whisker watcher. Every Sunday night, for as long as I could remember, she would carefully smooth a creamy, pale pink layer of Nair® across her upper lip and chin. I can still smell its clean, slightly blossomy scent. She'd calmly walk around with the familiar mask, and then remove it, as per the directions, after about eight minutes. A little face cream to cool the skin. She would then be whisker-free for another week.

How is it you can have chemotherapy, lose an entire head of hair,

> ## Not the maker of plans and promises, but rather the one who offers faithful service in small matters...this is the person who is most likely to achieve what is good and lasting.
>
> — *Johann Wolfgang von Goethe*
> *(1749-1832)*

and still have chin hairs?! It is because of this type of irony that this pact is important. Through the final stage of her illness, we continued to apply the Nair®.

Then about two days before she died, she became extremely quiet. She couldn't speak, due to the heaviness of the morphine, but was in no pain. I was fussing with her—taking her blood pressure, turning her, administering the morphine. And suddenly I noticed... the whiskers!

Out came the Nair®. Applied around the mouth and chin. Careful timing so as not to burn the skin. Gentle removal with a tissue and application of some soothing cream. As I finished the process, I softly said to her, "Rita, I removed your whiskers."

Incredibly, amazingly, and stunningly to me, she smiled.

I knew, then, she was there, and that she knew I'd kept my promise: to take care of her and to see to her most personal needs. That's what "whisker watch" was about. Keeping my word. Doing what she asked—no matter how absurd it might appear to another, given the state of affairs.

Promises made between two people can be deeply intimate and personal affairs. If there is ever a time to slip away from a promise, it's when no one is looking. Yet, who knows who might be watching?

Honoring people in our lives means making a commitment that

extends beyond their immediate presence. I had truly thought my mother was absent from me in that moment. But she was there, and her smile was such a gift—a reminder that what she told me was important to her really mattered.

Honor is deeply personal. I know that the one who must watch my promises is me. The one who best knows your character and the value of your word is you. Your actions will either confirm or deny your intent. So be careful whose "whiskers" you promise to remove. It's a great responsibility you take on when you pledge your faithfulness to another in his or her time of need.

Need looks like different things to different people. A child never understands how a big business meeting can be more important than a recital you promised to attend. An employee can't appreciate that you're under so many deadlines you forgot to acknowledge an achievement the way you should have. And those you love have trouble forgiving you when it seems you've just made a bad decision because your "x" means more than their "y."

Your word is your bond. Make it so. And realize that a promise to another is truly a promise to yourself.

Your Own Wisdom:

Courage

Stop Trying to Be Something You're Not

Dead Rita's Wisdom:
Who you are works, and
it's wonderful.

$\mathcal{W}$HEN I WAS YOUNG I was really clear about who I wanted to be: my mother.

I don't remember a time when I didn't like her. I never went through a stage in high school when I hated her. Frankly, I wasn't too sympathetic with friends who were disgusted with their parents. I didn't get it.

I certainly wasn't the perfect teenager. I went through a serious boy-crazy phase, during which I thought Rita would have a stroke. But I always showed her great respect and kept most of my boy-crazy behaviors out of sight.

From a very early age, there were only two things I wanted to do: talk and eat. (Truly not much has changed.) I was chunky, would talk to anyone, and had no trouble sharing everything I heard in the house with my neighbors. My sense of humor came from my dad, who is one of the funniest people I will ever know. He was a cross between Fred Flintstone, Jackie Gleason, and Archie Bunker. He would say the most outrageous things—and laugh like a hyena at his own jokes. I was right there, guffawing with him.

I was loud and funny. I was a girl's girl, but my mouth would spew the most amazing things. Things that Rita would *never* say. She would "suck wind" in shock—and then laugh. She appreciated my verve and courage and was always struck by my ability to try anything—qualities she lacked, simply because no one had ever encouraged her.

But I dreamed of being different. Of being demure and petite and ladylike. Of being like my mother.

Rita was a perfect size four. I was a less-than-perfect size fourteen. Clothes looked amazing on her. And she was always put together. She never chided me about my weight, but I dreamed of wearing her clothes. Rita: five feet, four inches, petite. Me: five feet, five-and-three-quarters inches, husky. I was simply taller and bigger. And oh, the pain I felt.

I always told Rita that I wanted to be just like her. She'd say, "No Vic, I wouldn't wish that on you." But I didn't care—I knew what I knew. Perfection lay in becoming like Rita, my role model.

I carried the shame of not being demure and petite and ladylike. But you certainly couldn't tell my shame—not by my actions, my words, or my eating habits. As I grew older, I enjoyed success, a happy marriage, and wonderful friends. Other people often told me how much they admired me. And yet... and yet...

One day when I was thirty-nine, I said something *extremely* outrageous, even by my standards. I was mortified. Who better to talk to than Rita? When I told her what I'd said, laughing and shaking my head, she roared with laughter.

"Mother," I said, "what am I going to do? Why do I say such things?"

She quieted down and looked at me. "Vicky, stop trying to be something you're not. Who you are works, and it's wonderful."

Even though I'd always had my mother's approval and support, and even though she'd said those same words to me in the past, I finally heard them. Really heard them.

For the first time in my life, I stopped wanting to be demure and petite and ladylike.

I began wanting to be me.

It's enough to be who we are. It's enough to step into our own fullness and examine the gifts we've been given. It's enough to embrace our greatness and not chase the spotlight of another.

Chasing the spotlight. That's what I'd been doing. Standing on the stage of Rita's life, hoping and praying that one day I would magically become her. Meanwhile, all of the people in my life who were watching me on my own stage just wanted me to be myself.

How often do we define ourselves through someone else? In a

family, sibling rivalry can intensify with age. In business, what we've done is never good enough by our own standards. In love, we often seek relationships that don't honestly reflect and support who we really are. There can be a level of frustration that underlies all of our success and accomplishments, until that moment when we realize we must stop trying to be something we're not.

After those words of wisdom from Rita—which I'd chosen to hear for the first time—I began to use my gifts more effectively. The power to say outrageous things became the power to say things with such passion and purpose that few people doubt my position. I'm fearless—not fearful like Mother was. And I understand now that this fearfulness was some of the reason for her demureness. She would choose not to say things out of fear. She was highly opinionated, very curious, always questioned different views—just not often publicly. Rather, she expressed her views to her outrageous, outspoken daughter.

That day, when I gave myself permission and the freedom to be *me* with all my beauty and warts, was a day that changed me forever. The only thing that changed was the faith I suddenly had that I could be me. That it was okay to be me. And frankly, "me" does work.

If you doubt that who you are is enough as you're standing on your life's stage, and you're looking in the wings for direction, stop. Begin again by looking out at your life, your audience. Recognize and accept the approval of those who see your best and want more of it. Stop trying to be something you're not—and you'll define the "something" you are.

Your Own Wisdom:

I Don't Mean Maybe

Dead Rita's Wisdom:
Nothing can change your life
as much as standing your
ground.

*B*OTH MY PARENTS WORKED. When Rita got home at night, dead on her feet, my siblings and I would squawk at her like three impatient baby birds in the nest. "We're hungry! What's for dinner? Can we pleeease go to McDonald's?"

No one wanted that marvelous treat more than I did. I felt that we were justified in eating at what I knew, in my young life, to be the finest of restaurants. The benefit was clear: It would make dinner easy for Rita. But it was also the perfect reward. I'd protected my little brother from harm after school, there had been no visible bodily injury meted out between my older brother and me, and the house had not been completely upended before Mother's arrival home. So it made perfect sense.

Mother would be silent. She'd ignore us. The campaign would be on.

"No," she'd eventually respond to our begging. "I'll make dinner in a bit."

Wax beans were imminent (for some reason wax beans were a serious staple in our home).

The adrenaline would rise. The wheedling and cajoling would continue. Faster. Higher pitched. Game on!

Suddenly she'd grow tired of the whining and say, very seriously, "I said *no*, and I don't mean maybe!"

Match point. Game over. Dinner would be served in about an

hour. Not bad food—she was a great cook. But not McDonald's.

"I don't mean maybe" meant just that. Whatever had come before that statement was now irrevocable truth. Her yes was yes, and her no was no—though I never really believed it until those other words were uttered. Until they were said, the outcome of the game might still have changed.

I think it's part of a child's mission in life to break their parents' resolve about matters that are destined to go in what the child believes to be absolutely the wrong direction. To get their way. To change their parents' mind. To wheedle, cajole, convince. To beg for an answer different from the one they've been given.

It's the first way we learn the art of negotiation. As any parent will tell you, and as any child knows, decisions can change. Parents can be convinced to shift gears, give up, and abandon their resolve. That's a good day for a kid.

With great interest, I watch my grandchildren's ability to change their parents' minds. I remember parenting their parents—my stepchildren—and how changeable I sometimes proved to be in areas where I wanted to be resolute. After all, I was in my twenties raising teenagers; I knew it all. Then they would begin their relentless campaigns to turn me around—and often they'd win the day.

Yet there were those times when nothing could shake me from my position, when Dead Rita's phrase of choice would come forth: "I said *no*, and I don't mean maybe!"

I would laugh to myself when I said it. To be even a shadow of Rita as a parent was all that I ever hoped for. But the steely resolution my mother's wisdom planted in me truly served me well—just as it served the kids.

I don't think unyielding resolve should be used without just cause. Opinions should, at times, be open to discussion and change. But some things are absolutes. "No, you're not going to that party. I know there will be kids drinking and doing drugs. No. I said *no*. I don't mean maybe."

Match point. Game over.

Being able to say no when you mean no and yes when you mean yes is a strength in life. An external strength—an internal fortress.

When I can say *I don't mean maybe* in my own life, I know I am firm in my resolve, clear in my plan of action.

It's about resolve. Reaching a decision and holding to it, knowing what you know and being true to it.

Nothing can change your life as much as standing your ground. Do it incessantly or without giving thought to both sides, and you're simply being stubborn. But it can be a positive force to know what you believe and what you want for yourself or another, and then take a firm stand when the situation calls for it.

Where in your own life do you say to yourself, *I don't mean maybe*? Career, love, child-rearing, relationships, self-healing, dreams, goals, spirituality?

Or are you wishy-washy, easily swayed by anyone determined enough to change your mind?

Sometimes I think that *I don't mean maybe* can be a line in the sand, a place to begin, an awareness that you mean business.

More "I don't mean maybes" can change your life. Memories of ultimatums from Rita helped provide me with those bits of resolve when I needed them. If she'd said it a little more often in her own life, I believe she, too, would have found more success.

And (wait for it…) I don't mean maybe.

Your Own Wisdom:

A Peace I Can't Explain

Dead Rita's Wisdom:
Finding spiritual peace can
provide the greatest comfort.

HEN RITA WAS A YOUNG ADULT, she discovered and attended the Episcopal Church in Norwalk, Ohio. She went alone—faith was never a part of her parents' life. When my father came to Norwalk from New York, he began attending church with her. After they married, they continued to attend. Mother worked in the church office. They were a fine Christian family.

My grandmother, on the other hand, declared herself an agnostic and was in good company—her first cousin was Madelyn Murray O'Hair, the mother of all atheists. Another scandal for Rita to bear. A small town was no place to gain notoriety, and yet there was plenty to murmur about when it came to this family.

My father embraced the Episcopal Church as he did everything—with passion and fervor. Rita said she came to hate going to church with him. His self-righteousness became too much for her tastes, because she knew how hypocritically he lived his life. She was also, in the end, influenced by her mother, who had long ago discarded the notion of God and saw no need for Him. Over the years, Rita's church attendance dropped off, so by the time my younger brother was born, she stayed home while Dad continued to attend.

My father, older brother, and I went to church in Fort Wayne regularly. I loved attending with my father. I liked being close to God. My mother attended so rarely, joining us only for Easter and Christmas, that fellow churchgoers assumed my father was a widower.

Dead Rita saw her life as a reflection of errors she made. She rarely, if ever, spoke of a prayer life, but she was quite superstitious. If I asked her what she believed, she said she believed in God—but I never saw her faith give her any comfort. I think she prayed for us, but I don't remember her turning to God in crisis.

Personally, I could not go through life without my faith. There's no explanation for all that happens in this universe other than something or someone much greater than I being in control. Having experienced a deepening of faith at one point in my life, I did my fair share of witnessing to Rita.

"Mother, do you know Jesus Christ as your Lord and Savior?" I'd ask.

"No, Vicky, I don't need a middle man—I go directly to God."

We would lovingly, as always, agree to disagree. I always believed that peace could be hers for the asking. But she did not know peace.

Her absolute worst fear was cancer. Her beloved grandmother, the one person who gave and taught her unconditional love, died of brain cancer in the early 1960s. Rita forever mourned her loss. She was terrified of suffering the pain and loss of dignity she had seen her grandmother experience.

As life would have it, she got breast cancer. And she wouldn't use the "C" word. She refused to say "cancer."

She managed to face and beat the breast cancer. She was well for over a year. And then lung cancer struck in July 1997.

We were now in the big leagues, and she began to fight. She had given up with the breast cancer, not treating it for eighteen months. She was certain that it was a death sentence not worth the struggle, but when it didn't kill her, she changed. Now lung cancer had arrived, and she wanted to live. The chemo, the radiation, the exhaustion—she faced it all head-on.

At the same time, my dad was dancing his own dance with diabetes. He was losing his sight, and had had his leg removed while Rita was getting her breast removed. For me, it was one of the most challenging and interesting times in my life with both my parents. Dad got an artificial leg, fumbled and spilled everything with his increasing blindness, and raged against Rita even in her disease. But Rita didn't falter. She quietly decided to conquer her cancer. She even began to use the "C" word.

In fact, she began to thrive even as the cancer grew. It spread to her liver and brain. She became weaker and weaker. Yet she grew stronger and stronger, too. She had found peace—a peace like she had never known. She was gracious and funny and full of appreciation and love. I have never met a more modest woman; I had never seen her breasts until one was removed and I had to provide postoperative care. But she never lost her dignity or grace, even while losing all personal privacy in the course of her treatment.

The cancer was vicious. It robbed her of her strength, her breath, her art, her independence. But, curiously, it also gave her a sense of who she was in the world.

I prayed for her without ceasing, and God provided me tremendous focus during her illness. I didn't mourn the thought of losing her. We spent so much time together as I cared for her and oversaw her treatments. We were one during what proved to be a precious time. Yet I wondered about her spiritual beliefs. I needed to know that she would be in heaven—as I understood heaven to be.

The concern was clearly about me. She hated being preached to, and rarely responded when asked about God. So I didn't feel I could pursue it.

But one day she shared that something had happened. "You know, Vic," she said, "I have a peace that I can't explain, I can't put into words."

I was comforted—believing, finally, that she had found a centering within herself.

"Mom," I ventured, "have you accepted Christ as your Lord and Savior?"

She quietly said, "Vicky, I have no one but Christ to thank for all that has happened to me."

We never spoke of it again.

I don't know what heaven looks like—or if my particular faith is the only way. But I know that finding spiritual peace gave my mother comfort like I had never seen in her before. It truly was a peace that surpassed all understanding.

Finding faith is finding the "why" for so much. That message is often shouted loudest to us when we're in pain. In the end, that wisdom allowed my mother to live—and die—peacefully. Whatever your own path, open yourself to that sense of spirit and you may be surprised at what you gain in return.

Your Own Wisdom:

Leave Your Entire World

Dead Rita's Wisdom:
Unless you're willing to leave all you know for someone, they're not "the one."

I LOVE LOVE! I LOVE FALLING in love. I love attracting a man. And from the time I was a teenager until I got married, I had a very successful catch-and-release program going with the men in my life.

I never really wanted to get married. So I got engaged, formally and informally, about seven times.

It was Rita's fault. She provided me with the ultimate, infallible litmus test. Seven times, when I applied this test, I changed my mind about the upcoming nuptials. To the expectant groom I would say, "Sorry—I just don't think we can get married."

I was seventeen the first time I got engaged. He was a great guy, about five years older than I. He really loved me and I liked him a lot. I was struggling to figure out how I was going to go to college, and here was a guy that wanted me to be his wife. So in the summer of my eighteenth year, when he presented me with a lovely engagement ring—I accepted. I was figuratively headed down the aisle, and Rita was less than impressed.

It didn't take much, of course, for this man to find himself completely out of Rita's favor. Before long he was banished from the house—literally, not allowed inside. Our solution? He'd pick me up outside. Which Rita countered with a new rule: "He's not allowed in the driveway." So I'd walk to the street. "He's not allowed on our street!" We'd

Our wedding, August 15, 1981

meet at the corner. Until the final ultimatum: "It's him or us."

It was a stunning decision to have to make. In the end it wasn't much of a match. I liked the guy a lot—but it never occurred to me to pick him over my family. So I broke up with him. But I was furious that Rita had made me choose, and I told her so.

"How could you do that," I said. "How could you make me choose?"

Rita uttered maybe the best piece of wisdom she ever gave me: "Look. Someday you may choose someone we don't agree with. If you can leave your entire world to be with him, then go. If you can't, he's not the one."

We never discussed it again.

But that wisdom didn't end my catch-and-release program! I'd date a guy for awhile, then come home and announce that I was engaged. Some of my selections made Rita laugh out loud. In one instance, she laughed so hard she fell against the refrigerator. I became the family's running joke. Dad, never intending to pay for any of these heavenly love matches, would shout, "Call the caterer!" (We all loved the party planning aspects of the wedding. No one was thinking about the marriage.)

And so it went. Lots of great men in my life. Lots of love. Each time they'd "close the deal" with a request for my hand in marriage, I'd respond with a hearty, "Sure!" Then I'd go to a place in my heart to take the test. A test I knew would reveal true love.

"Would I leave my entire world to be with this man?" I would ask myself. The answer would always come back quickly: "Nah!"

Each time I'd say, "It's better if we don't get married. I'm not ready. I hope you understand." And I would bid adieu to my latest intended.

In 1980, I had just broken up with one of my informal fiancés. I was working forty hours a week and going to school for fifteen credit hours while dating lots of great men. Then John Trabosh came to Fort Wayne, Indiana, for a business meeting. Handsome. Older by eighteen years. Mature. Funny. Sexy. Smart. My kind of guy.

Then again, he was legally separated, with four children he was raising alone... he lived in a different city, two hundred miles away...

Impossible, yes. And a perfect set-up for my game of love.

We began to date. John's divorce was finalized and he got custody of his children. Our relationship grew, and I fell deeply in love. Again. With another great man. I think I was even the first to broach the subject of marriage, to which John responded with a cautious "Okay," not sure himself if it was a good idea. Yet we couldn't deny the amazing love we shared.

Amazing—and impossible. A man eighteen years older than I. Four kids. Living in a different city. Absolutely the least likely candidate for a husband for this twenty-two-year-old.

Rita's response to this love match? Incredulous. Unhappy. No falling against anything in laughter. She refused to meet John, and didn't want to talk about marriage. I was devastated. My best friend did not want to meet the man I loved—and she didn't. Not for eleven months. It broke my heart.

But I did not split up with him.

John and I moved forward with our plans, seeing each other as often as we could—every few weeks, over a weekend at best. I made the most of it; I knew I was in love. But finally, with my wedding just months away, with Mother wanting nothing to do with the plans, and feeling lonely, I found myself close to the end of my rope. I was beginning to lose hope.

It seemed time to break it off. Time to ask the question I had broached so many times before and that had set me free. Surely it would end this complicated relationship like it had so many others. Quietly I asked myself, *"Would I leave my entire world to be with this man?"*

> Love is everything it's
> cracked up to be. That's
> why people are so
> cynical about it…It really
> is worth fighting for,
> risking everything for.
> And the trouble is, if you
> don't risk everything,
> you risk even more.
>
> — *Erica Jong*

"*Yes,*" I found myself responding without hesitation.

I was astounded. *Unbelievable*, I thought. *He's the one. The impossible one.*

And so I continued. My friends, family, ex-boyfriends, faux fiancés … everyone was stunned. On I marched—through one of the loneliest periods of my life.

Mother and I never fought about my decision. She was never cruel. She simply said, "You're making a mistake, Vicky. You shouldn't marry him." I replied that I was going to—and never told her she was the one who'd given me the means, the wisdom to know that he was the one.

As deeply as I loved my life and family, I was willing to risk it all to be with John.

We were married on August 15, 1981. It was not an especially happy day for me, not the day I had hoped it would be. It was a very small, modest wedding. There was no great joy from my darling mother. And it began a life that I could not imagine. Becoming an instant parent of four kids, two living with us, two on the East Coast, moving to Cleveland, starting a new career, leaving all I knew and loved.

But I did it. And all of Rita's wisdom sustained me.

Her doubting that I could do it gave me my resolve. I didn't call her when I was tearing my hair out. I didn't want to hear, "Come back home, you don't need this." I knew that if I had an easy out, I just might take it. It was her doubt that strengthened me. I remembered how well she had parented and I tried my best to do the same with my new stepchildren.

And we made it. John and I celebrated our first wedding anniversary in Oregon. I was now geographically farther away from my mother than I could have ever imagined, yet we never lost touch. We wrote and called constantly. And then one day she said, "You know Vic, I was wrong. You and John do belong together."

It was then that I reminded her of the wisdom she had given me at seventeen when she made me choose between a boyfriend and my world. I told her how I had applied it each time since—and that no one but John had passed the test.

She didn't recall having said what she did—and isn't that how wisdom often works?

We rarely know how what we say will affect another. I've shared this favorite piece of Rita's advice with many women and men. Know that unless you're willing to leave all you know for someone, they're not "the one." Date away! Explore lots of relationships. Fully committing to someone means that you'll work harder to make the relationship successful than you can imagine. And why do it for anyone other than someone for whom you would give your all?

Marriage and commitment are the hardest things I have ever done. Nothing is more frustrating, challenging, and full of compromise than this intimate relationship. And nothing brings greater joy.

I have Dead Rita to thank for that. When you're willing to leave your whole world for this kind of love, and you make that commitment, you realize you won't lose your world—instead, this love will complete your world.

To be willing to lose your world is to gain everything. Give this wisdom some serious consideration.

Your Own Wisdom:

Clean Your House Before You Go on Vacation

Dead Rita's Wisdom:
Cleaning things up can be
a gift to ourselves.

*R*ITA WAS A GREAT HOUSEKEEPER. She had the whole house-wife thing down cold. Even with a typical husband and three messy children, our house still looked great.

Whenever I attempted to clean the areas assigned to me, it was never clean enough. She was picky. And I was a bored teenager.

Because she worked full-time she would kill herself cleaning the house on the weekend. I'd help—but in the way that makes an exasperated parent say, "Oh let me show you!" And show me she would.

"Nice job, Mom!"

What really drove me crazy was her insistence on cleaning the house from stem to stern before we went on vacation. I hated it, because everyone was expected to pitch in—no one more than I. It was a ritual that made no sense to me. But she would not be dissuaded, no matter how hard I tried.

"Who cares what the house looks like?" I'd say. "We're not going to be here!"

But Rita would explain that when she returned from any vacation the last thing she wanted to face was a mess. In the end, this same mentality carried over into my own life.

I lack the cleaning gene that Dead Rita had. I love a clean house—I just don't love cleaning it. My family and I aren't slobs, but we definitely never met Rita's standards.

When my parents lived with us, one of the many joys I experienced was Rita's insistence on cleaning our house, since I refused to accept her offer of rent. "Knock yourself out," I thought. And she did. Twice a week she'd go through the place, cleaning the floor on her hands and knees—and she loved it. She was contributing in a way that meant something to her. Who was I to deny her this pleasure?

So I had this great role model. But following her example always proved a bit difficult for me. That clean gene thing just passed me by. It did, however, affect my work life.

I operate in a state of organized chaos. Lots of piles, lots of papers, lots of projects. Looks kinda messy. No worries... all will be organized later. But later rarely comes.

Until, that is, a vacation looms. And then Rita's words come back—now so clearly wise to me. "Clean your house before you go on vacation."

I cannot imagine leaving my day-to-day office mess and walking out the door for a couple of weeks. What if my staff needed something? I could find it in the great pyramids of paper in a second, but they would have to organize a search party. And what if, God forbid, I died on vacation? What would people think? "We miss her, but she was a slob."

Every time I prepare to leave my daily routine behind, I'm motivated by my desire to have others think well of me in my absence. I can see them all at the funeral, weeping, shaking their heads in sadness—noting how much quieter the world will be without me... and what a fantastic businesswoman I was. And how organized I was!

This would not be possible if I left a mess.

If a vacation is on the horizon (like tomorrow's horizon), piles that usually seem to grow are handled. Extraordinary amounts of work are accomplished. After all, there is no tomorrow to do it in—tomorrow is a plane at six a.m. whisking me off to warmer climes.

Fantastic numbers of decisions are made, papers filed, tasks assigned, and projects completed.

I call it my death mentality: "They're not going to catch me dead with a mess!" I'm "cleaning my house" when I prepare to take off. And the exhilaration that comes with having done the work! The sense of peace and satisfaction.

What would it take to live this way, always?

I have no idea. There are so many factors that kick in with a vacation deadline. Adrenaline, competition with myself, the thought of the embarrassment if needs arise while I'm gone—or am suddenly "gone." Enough to make things happen for sure!

Whatever the case, all this comes from Dead Rita's wisdom about cleaning her house. Of course, it's great wisdom to clean it up, make a fresh start, leave without concern, and enjoy the vacation.

As I return to my office after a great trip, it's shiny clean except for the stacks of new mail and decisions carefully laid out by staff. No problem—I'm relaxed, refreshed, renewed, refocused.

Cleaning our house, whether literally or figuratively, can have those outcomes. When my office gets too noisy with papers, I stop and clean it out. Visual chaos saps creative energies, and in my case, this can make me feel bad about who I am. I don't want to feel bad. I want success. Don't you? There are times when cleaning things up can be a gift to ourselves.

If we're not wise enough to make that choice in the moment, with any luck there's always another vacation just around the corner! Or, take a moment to imagine a vacation and give yourself a tough deadline. "Three hours to clean this up—and then ... Tahiti!!" (virtual Tahiti). It's a game—a goal. But when you're through, you can leave satisfied and begin anew, afresh, tomorrow.

Your Own Wisdom:

I Couldn't Care Less

Dead Rita's Wisdom:
Why care what others
think when their opinions
don't matter?

*R*ITA LOVED THE ENGLISH LANGUAGE. She studied it. She loved to write. Though she didn't make it beyond high school, she continued to learn, wanting to lift herself from her self-imposed stigma of not graduating from college.

In a truly daring move for her, she took a writing class at the Indiana University – Purdue University extension in Fort Wayne. She was in heaven. She wrote short stories and would sit in terror as they were read out loud in class by the instructor. The praise she then received was almost more than her soul could embrace.

Like many tortured artists, she created her stories in spite of her belief that she was nothing but an impostor. Now that's torture. Not knowing who you are. Not knowing what you know. But the two people my mother should have been able to trust with her dreams continually blindsided her. The source of their ill temper and angst remains a mystery. Whatever the reason, my grandmother and father made Rita a target for their unhappiness in life, and she took full-on their blows of subtle and not-so-subtle remarks—which were devastating to her.

Yet if anyone told her something that she knew was untrue about another, that person's opinion would be met with a simple, "I couldn't care less."

This particular expression is often misquoted. It drove her crazy.

She'd hear someone say, "I could care less!" and she'd be off. "If they could care less, then why do they bother to say so?" she'd argue passionately. "It's 'I couldn't care less!' Which is why you say it!"

She found poor English a sign of ignorance—reflecting her own fear of being ignorant. Even colloquialisms made her uncomfortable. To me this was a sign of her insecurity, since colloquialisms are part of the English lexicon. Her formality of speech would at times make others think she was standoffish, though she was, in truth, simply shy and afraid to look dumb.

She taught me to say I couldn't care less when I'd hear something hurtful or untrue, or meant to undermine me. I'd share an experience with her and she'd say, "You tell them that you couldn't care less what they think."

The most opportune times came in high school. In the mid-1970s, drug use was picking up steam. I had great friends, some of whom were experimenting. Never my thing. I don't like being out of control, and drugs and alcohol definitely take things out of my control.

As a senior, I tried alcohol to excess at a particularly memorable party, but I got so sick and so drunk that it was my last foray into that world for some time. Drugs were always being offered and there was the typical peer pressure. But I always said no.

I never actually uttered "I couldn't care less" in these situations. I simply felt it.

I couldn't care less what my friends thought of my lack of interest in getting high. Really couldn't care less. That was the strength of Dead Rita's wisdom. Why care what others think when their opinion about a certain matter is irrelevant to your life, goals, dreams, and beliefs?

This was further enforced by my own interpretation of a great quote I read in *The Fountainhead* by Ayn Rand. Howard Roark, the story's protagonist, is an architect who would rather struggle in obscurity than compromise his artistic and personal vision. He faces other characters who are bent on destroying him. His enemy, Ellsworth Toohey, is a columnist intent on becoming the victor in any encounter with Roark. In their only face-to-face encounter in the book, Toohey says to Roark, "Why don't you tell me what you think of me, Mr. Roark?" Roark replies, "But I don't think of you."

I read this at age eighteen. Then and now, I am deeply affected by the profundity of that level of following your own path, rather than being consumed by those around you. While I don't embrace Rand's philosophies regarding objectivism, there is wisdom in not caring for another's opinions simply because we must. There's wisdom in believing that we're complete even without the collective approval of the world. Had Rita been able to take that fully to heart, she may have been able to break free of those who held her back with their own issues and pain.

Greatness comes from caring passionately about what matters most to us. Greatness is hampered when we believe that we must be validated by others for our greatness to count. To grow as a person, we must have the ability to know and differentiate "great" from "good enough." But remember Dead Rita's Wisdom: There are those moments when you shouldn't care less what others think—because you are in a moment of greatness, and you know it.

Your Own Wisdom:

March Seventeenth

Dead Rita's Wisdom:
Come full circle.

*T*HE FIRST TIME I REMEMBER ever seeing my mother cry was the day we buried her grandmother.

Standing there at the cemetery, about four years of age, I watched my mother weep. To see her so bereft was more than my heart could bear. As if we were connected, I felt my own tears begin to flow. From that moment on until the day she died, if Mother cried, I cried.

Rita had deeply loved Anna, her maternal grandmother, and the love was returned tenfold. When Anna Ward died of brain cancer in 1961 at the age of sixty-eight, having suffered terribly in the course of her disease, it completely devastated Rita.

Anna passed away on March seventeenth. Rita mourned on that day for the rest of her life. When I was young I'd sometimes forget the date, as kids do, and then become aware of a subtle sadness in my mother. When I'd ask her what was wrong, she would remind me, "This is the day that Gram died." Over the years it became special to me as well.

I didn't know Anna well, yet I always felt a connection with her— I felt her deep in my heart. So much so that when I met John, my husband-to-be, and thought about having children, I once experienced a vision—incredibly real—of a little girl I would one day have. A daughter named Anna Clark, after Anna Ward and Rita Clark Ho-

Rita, 1955

ering. I had never really wanted children. But somehow the image was unshakable; little "Annie" would not go away. I carried her with me for years.

Anna. She was Rita's lifeline in the midst of all the chaos of her childhood. Growing up, my mother had an extremely dysfunctional life. She dealt with yelling, physical fights, anger. Though she never mentioned having been struck, the verbal abuse from her parents was world class. When people hear her life story, they wonder how she ever came out in one piece. Raising us, she consciously strove to stop the abuse she'd suffered.

In the early 1990s I visited Rita in Fort Wayne, Indiana, before she moved to Oregon. We found ourselves discussing how she'd managed to maintain her sanity in spite of her upbringing. She was such a wonderful, nurturing mother. I couldn't help but wonder how she'd instinctively known how to do it. She certainly hadn't learned at her own mother's knee. By this time, Loretta had moved to Fort Wayne, and Rita was visiting her every day. She'd kept it up for years. Yet my grandmother was never satisfied. Rita felt forever guilty, and there was no joy in her desperate attempt to gain her mother's approval.

So I began asking Rita about her grandmother Anna. As she lovingly described this woman, easily twenty-five years after her death, I had a revelation. "Mom," I said, "your Gram was your mother! Not in a physical sense. But she represented everything a mother should be, and she taught you unconditional love. She was the one who saved you!"

And Mother agreed.

This connection, this woman that my mother could never forget, was the "why"—the reason Rita had become the woman she had. Taking what her grandmother provided—her love and support— Rita had made it her own, became her own person. Her own wise, fine and wonderful self.

With our conversation, a certain weight seemed to lift from Mother as she continued to make those daily visits to the unresponsive Loretta. And with the epiphany we shared, the little girl "Annie" faded from my head and heart. I realized that she had been there all those many years leading me to explore, with Rita, her path. To discover how she'd made it to the best part of herself. It was as if the spirit of my great-grandmother was just waiting for me to help Rita find peace. Even after death, she'd been there for her beloved granddaughter. I wasn't meant to have an "Annie"—John and I never had children together. But I love and am so grateful to my great-grandmother—the Anna in my past.

From that day on, I never forgot March seventeenth.

In the last few months of Rita's life, we had to plan her funeral. She and I were not crazy about the idea, but we were women of action. The funeral director met with us at the house and we discussed details of the funeral. After she left, I delicately asked Mother where she wanted to be buried. "Not with your father," she retorted, which made us both laugh hysterically. She had decided to be cremated, and I asked, "Well, what should I do with your ashes?"

"Oh, split 'em up between you three kids," she replied.

Then I quietly said, "What if I buried you with your grandmother in Norwalk?"

She began to cry. And then, of course, I cried as well. She said how wonderful that would be.

My mother died on October third. I decided I would take her ashes back to her beloved Norwalk, Ohio, and bury her on the following March seventeenth. When the day came, my brother Jeff, who lived in Fort Wayne, met me in Norwalk. I was concerned about the weather—there had been a blizzard with fourteen inches of snow just the week before. But the day was of utmost importance—no matter the weather.

> Missing someone
> isn't about how long
> it has been since
> you've seen them or
> the amount of time
> since you've talked.
> It's about the very
> moment when you're
> doing something and
> wishing they were
> right there with you.
>
> — *Unknown*

I contacted a few of her old high school chums who still lived in Norwalk. Not knowing she had died, they were quick to want to honor her. I contacted the Salvation Army, who sent a lovely woman pastor.

We went to the cemetery. The weather was overcast; the ground was covered with snow. We decided to hold a small ceremony at the gravesite and later the workers would place Rita's ashes in Anna's casket. It was thirty-eight years earlier, to the day, that I stood in the same place watching Rita weep upon losing her beloved grandmother.

There was a miracle here, as a boombox played a hymn while the six of us gathered around Anna's grave. The miracle was how sad yet how truly peaceful we all were. There had been a blizzard the week before. The snow was still thick on the ground. But the sun had come out that day and by the time we held our modest service, only the snow on my great-grandmother's grave had melted. I looked around and wondered what this miracle was about. I then remembered asking God for a sign that burying Mom here was the right thing to do. And this little gravesite, void of snow, stopped me from wondering. It was a moment where I swear, if God could talk, He was gently saying, "How's this?"

It had all come full circle. The significance of March seventeenth was never to be lost on me. Rita's unerring honor for her grandmother each March seventeenth—her grounding force—was perfect, in that it would now honor her as well. There are dates that hold tremendous significance. Our memories allow our love to be securely tucked away. On those special days we again remember what we never want to forget. Comfort and grief are our companions. Together they can sustain us—and remind us how fortunate we have been to love or be loved.

Your Own Wisdom:

Communication

You Do Too Much

Dead Rita's Wisdom:
Too much is plainly too much.

ITA WATCHED ME GO A million miles an hour for years. I've always been driven. Always had big goals. And I've been quite the procrastinator. I get a lot of energy from hitting a deadline, but the deadline must often be looming for it to become a catalyst. When you're interested in many things and you have many diverse abilities, when you're a procrastinator and your greatest joy is other people, you can create chaos, often more internal than external.

When I was young and attending college, I found that simply going to school bored me. I didn't love to study—I wanted to work. So I left the Purdue campus, returned home, found a full-time job, and then added twelve credit hours at the Indiana University-Purdue University extension in Fort Wayne. It seemed just about right.

I was crazed. By semester finals I was so tired and stressed that I thought I was going to have a mental breakdown. And I wasn't always successful. I didn't always pass all of my classes and so I would have to retake them. Some semesters I blew off entirely and just worked sixty hours a week instead. It took me six years to get my bachelor's degree. It was a miracle that I got it at all.

Mother watched me. She would shake her head and say, "You do too much." I would just ignore her, and continue doing too much: Too much working. Too much talking. Too much spending money.

Too much saying yes to others' requests.

Thirty years later, I hear the same thing from those I love. Friends. Family. Husband. "You do too much." And I ask, how much is too much? Perhaps the answer was best expressed by writer Douglas Noel Adams: "If it looks like a duck, and quacks like a duck, we have at least to consider the possibility that we have a small aquatic bird of the family anatidae on our hands."

I am the duck. The duck that does too much.

It doesn't seem to work as well as I think it should. Because I hear from too many others, too often, that what I do is too much. Too much for them, but not for me? No. Too much, period.

If what we do is done well, it doesn't become a burden for others. But if my life's work is judged consistently as "too much"—even if just by appearance—then it's too much.

There are things I do that make it appear that it's too much for me. I appear too tired, I don't have time for friendships and family, my bigger calling takes from those who never wanted a bigger calling for me—they just wanted me. So is it the balance in my life I need to change? Or do I need to acknowledge what doesn't work, and decide that it's not an all-or-nothing world?

Perhaps it's about knowing what we want most, and what we're willing to give up to get it.

You do too much.

Ringing any bells? Sound familiar?

It's not necessary to do too much. It's necessary to do enough. As Rita would say, "Enough is enough." Maybe that's the balance. Enough.

For each area of your life there is enough. Enough food. Enough love. Enough friendship. Enough money. Enough success. Enough faith. Enough.

Too much is too much. Enough is enough.

Too much does not serve. This life is a marathon, hopefully a very long one. Sprinting through activities, through days, through projects that leave you breathing hard and in pain doesn't impress the onlookers. They're just left muttering, "You do too much." A hollow victory at best.

Balance may be found in doing things that most honor your values. These can help us define what "too much" looks like for us. For example, you value your family and children but don't spend time with them, because work calls. It's too much. You value a good organization, but don't delegate and so you burn out. It's too much.

Put the work away. Delegate tasks. Otherwise, consider what you—and others— lose, rather than gain.

It takes courage to hear the gentle truth that you're doing too much. Facing this truth means retraining our behaviors. It takes great wisdom to own up to the fact that too much is plainly too much. Any self-righteous reply of, "What do they know?" is simply foolishness.

Stop doing too much. Do *enough*. And then you and the Dead Ritas of your life will say that it was just right.

Your Own Wisdom:

Consider the Source

Dead Rita's Wisdom:
The intention of the person
speaking the words is
as important as the actual
words spoken.

S CHOOL ALWAYS HELD ITS CHALLENGES for me. I was outspoken and confident. But I could also be a little overbearing. A chubby child, I was a target for teasing, and I've always been extremely sensitive.

I covered my shyness with humor—I was the funny fat kid. But Mother always heard my truths and saw my pain. And she believed in me.

When someone said something cruel, I'd tell Rita. It wasn't a constant problem, but whenever someone was unkind for unkindness' sake, she would say, "Consider the source."

Consider the source. Said in certain tones, the phrase can smack of superiority. But Rita used it in a powerful way: to disregard the opinions of those whose only purpose was to put another person down, whose only purpose was to hurt someone who did not deserve unkindness. It always brought perspective. Through the years, that saying has kept me steady.

What do we choose to believe about ourselves? We choose to believe what we know to be true, what we're told by others, or a combination of the two. I've gotten to know and accept myself so well that what others say about me now is either a clear confirmation of what I already know, or it's something I can simply reject as untrue.

When we're not steadfastly aware of who and where we are in the

> To free us from
> the expectations
> of others, to
> give us back to
> ourselves—there
> lies the great,
> singular power
> of self-respect.
>
> — *Joan Didion*

world, we can become like a ship pitchpoling in the waves. Pitchpoling is the most dangerous way a boat can capsize—its stern lifts high in the air and its bow dives deeply into the back of the swell before it, flipping the boat over. Rocking violently in the waves, the ship will capsize and sink—regardless of its size.

If everyone else's opinions become your ocean, you'll soon be pitchpoling in the waves of your life, capsized by a particularly challenging swell.

As they say, if one person tells you that you have a green tail, they're crazy. If two people tell you that you have a green tail, it's a conspiracy. If *three* people tell you that you have a green tail, turn around and look!

My latest green tail? *You're doing too much.* I could "consider the source" and reject the comment. But it's not so easy when you're constantly hearing this comment—like I am right now. So I don't rebuff the observation—this wisdom—from people who care for me. These are not the words of those who want to see me fail.

Consider the source. There are those who don't have your best interests in mind. There are those who lace their comments with phrases and statements meant to trigger a reaction, not a response. Begin to look at those individuals and evaluate whether they really should be in your life.

Consider those who care for you as well. Consider who you would be without those who are willing to tell you the truth for your own good. Bless the messenger who cares enough to care enough.

And in your interactions with others, remember the same. Consider your intent and delivery in the comments you make. My mother never said things to hurt or degrade me. Be like Dead Rita in making sure no one in your life feels the need to "consider the source" when you become involved.

Your Own Wisdom:

Eyes in the Back of Your Head

Dead Rita's Wisdom:
Listen to your gut instinct,
and know that you know
what you know.

*R*ITA HAD EYES IN THE back of her head. She said so, but more importantly, she proved it.

She always seemed to know what was really going on. A few well-placed questions when I was a little girl, and I'd spill my guts. When I asked her how she knew, she'd simply say, "I have eyes in the back of my head." A little creepy, but more than anything, seriously intimidating! So I kept no secrets from her, not only because of the eyeball issue but for a number of reasons: One, why keep secrets from someone who loved me so much? Why not embrace her wisdom? And two, the pressure to spill was excruciating for one so young.

As I grew older, I knew she was wise. But there were also certain secrets I began to want to keep from her—mostly having to do with relationships with boys and then men. They were secrets that inevitably harmed me. Keeping the wrong secrets for the wrong reasons can do just that to a young woman. But Rita was chaste, virginal, and extremely private about all matters sexual. Not a great source of wisdom for an only daughter with no one else to talk to about the natural process of sexuality. Even normally developing sexual feelings were not acknowledged.

To compound the problem, I was well-developed by thirteen and attracted older men. That's fairly confusing when boys your own age don't seem the least bit interested. But Mother was my singular resource. My school of non-learning. So there were things it seemed better to keep to myself.

Still, her power of intuition was clear when I began to date a very special guy—special in that he was not like anyone I'd ever met.

As a high school senior, I worked in a fast food restaurant along with the rest of my friends. When I came to work one day, there stood before me a magnificent specimen of a *man*. Dark, handsome, mustached, and *working at my store flipping burgers*! I knew, in that moment, that there was a God.

We locked eyes, he slyly grinned, and I turned inside out.

"Who is that?" I breathlessly asked my girlfriend.

She said, "Oh, that's Jack. He's twenty-eight and just got out of prison."

"For what?" I asked.

"Drug dealing."

Oooh! I was not a girl to experiment with drugs, but it was undeniably interesting and very exciting. This was love. Jack began circling me like a cat playing with a mouse. Soon we were a couple.

I learned that he was a serial criminal and had enjoyed his fair share of time inside prison walls, having spent the majority of his adolescence and twenties locked up. He still lived with his mother, had never learned to drive (the closest he'd been to most cars was making license plates). Not especially bright, not especially kind, he was willing to talk to me, telling me everything I wanted to hear to get what he wanted from me. It worked like a charm. It was even *more* exciting when he began to introduce me to all of his friends who were ex-cons. They couldn't believe he'd landed this sweet young thing.

While the excitement continued, I also felt a fair amount of trepidation. Rita's constant talk of "nice boys want nice girls" niggled at me. Where was this going to lead? I had dreams of college and a career. Jack had dreams of drugs and his "old lady"—which, I kid you not, he began to call me.

Since Rita was my barometer for all things important, it came time for her to meet Jack. I warned him to be very careful around her, trying to impress on him that she would ferret out the truth about his criminal record, and then *we* would be over.

On the appointed day, he walked the three miles to our house.

Mother and boyfriend shared a polite conversation and smoked a few cigarettes together. Eventually Jack walked out of the house and began the walk home. A brilliantly successful first meeting, I thought. Maybe he knew nothing of what was happening in the world—he wasn't a big reader in prison, I assumed. But by my standards, he'd faked it well.

I turned to Rita. "Well," I asked expectantly, "what do you think of Jack?"

She paused and then said, "He's okay. But there's something wrong. It's like he's been... away, or something..."

If I'd had a weak heart, I'd have seized up like an old car engine and died on the spot. Instead, I looked at her, aghast. Feeling truly convicted, the words tumbled out.

"Oh, Mother! He's an ex-con. He's just got out of prison after eight years!"

She looked at me wide-eyed and burst out laughing. Then she said more to herself than to me, "I just knew he'd been away."

The lecture came, of course, and the truth came out that I needed to get away from him. That he was bad news. It's what I had instinctively known—but had chosen not to listen to. I broke up with him shortly after that. That was my first and last foray into the world of bad, bad boys.

Dead Rita's instinct was so good that she never questioned it. As a result, she always offered me her advice without hesitation and without over-thinking it. I have learned to do that for myself. I may not always be right, but most of the time I am. I believe our intuition, our internal knowledge, is right there waiting to be tapped. If we listen to it, there lies all the wisdom we need in the moment.

Use those eyes in the back of your head. Do you see what you see? Listen to that gut instinct. Do you argue with the internal truth or see it for the great GPS system that it is? If you just know that you know what you know, you, too can bring great wisdom to the world.

Your Own Wisdom:

You Make a Better Door Than a Window

Dead Rita's Wisdom:
It's a gift to be transparent
to someone who loves you.

*T*ELEVISIONS WERE VERY SMALL IN the 1960s. If I stood in the wrong place, usually in front of the TV, my mother would say, "You make a better door than a window."

I would immediately move. I got her point—I was acting as a door because no one could see through me.

How often did I think someone could understand or "see" what I was thinking? I made assumptions about their understanding of me, their knowledge of where I was coming from. In fact, none of those assumptions were true. No one can tell what I'm thinking unless I tell them. But when you communicate—express—you become a window rather than a door.

So much of our communication is lost in what we choose not to say—what we withhold, distort, or simply give up before we're understood. Our greatness is often lost because we fail to be clear, transparent, and understood.

You make a better door than a window. In the physical sense, this phrase is absolutely true. But in communication, we can choose to be crystal clear like a window, or closed like a door.

Often, words are inadequate to describe how I feel. Still, I must continue to put emotions into words. No one can read me, see through me, and be as accurate in their description of me as I can when I express what I know to be true about myself.

> Life is filigree work. What is written clearly is not worth much, it's the transparency that counts.
>
> — *Louis-Ferdinand Celine*

I become a door at times when I attempt to describe my sense of loss about Dead Rita. My grief is not overwhelming, but it is complicated. I am a person of accomplishment due, in large part, to a woman who gave me the wisdom I needed, just when I needed it. The part of me that is her can be remembered if I can somehow express the value of her wisdom and share it with others. When I become the window, she becomes alive once more. Not only for me, but for the listener.

If you believe that words are inadequate to describe feelings, you may be right. But you can reach another with your feelings when you learn to communicate, through tools and books and the example of another's words and prose. You can become the window when you choose to communicate and help others do the same.

Dead Rita opened herself to me. To almost all others, she was a closed door. She was so private. Well, that's over now! I hope that I'm using the gift she gave me for good—to allow others to open themselves up so that they can bring the kind of inspiration to another that Rita continues to bring to me.

So many of us feel inadequate to give inspiration to another. Dead Rita was truly an ordinary woman who accomplished something extraordinary—she allowed her full glory to be exposed to me, and I could do nothing but look and learn.

Visually to me, Mom always looked perfect—hair, nails, clothes, everything. Especially her hair—it was always in a perfect bouffant, or whatever the style was at the time. When she'd come home for lunch, she would catch me staring at her hair. She'd ask what I was staring at, and I would say, "Nothing."

She would just laugh. She could certainly see through me, yet she allowed me to love her so fully and joyfully. Because she allowed and appreciated my love, I experienced a sense of certainty that has given me a lifelong ability to love deeply and freely.

For me, Rita was not the door. She was the window. The communication we shared still sustains me to this day. What a gift it is to be transparent to someone who loves you. This gift, while freely given, must be carefully given. If she had ever trampled on my heart, I certainly wouldn't be inspired to speak and write about her. And the power of her words touches many because of who she was to me.

For whom are you the door? The window? How are you perceived by those with whom you work and play? And by those you love? Carefully examine what closes you down and what opens you up. Begin by honoring yourself and you will honor those around you.

Your Own Wisdom:

Cats for to Make Kitten Britches

Dead Rita's Wisdom: Sometimes our search for wisdom is more complicated than it needs to be.

I DIDN'T ASK "WHY?" A LOT when I was a little kid, but for whatever reason, I did ask, "What for?" Apparently, it was my variation on every kid's favorite question for just about everything.

Whenever I asked Rita, "What for?" she'd respond with, "Cats for." To which I'd automatically say, "Cats for?" And she'd laughingly say, "Cats for to make kitten britches!"

I never knew what that meant. She'd just laugh and wouldn't explain.

When I began to write down some of Dead Rita's Wisdom, "cats for to make kitten britches" bubbled up. Still not having the foggiest idea what it meant, my first thought was that there was no wisdom to be found in the saying. But, in the new tradition, I Googled the phrase. And voilà! Multiple links and posts immediately sprang up.

The expression is an old regional play on words. In response to the question "What fer?" (versus "What for?") the answer would be, "Cat's fur to make kitten britches!" Some of Dead Rita's relatives would have easily slipped into pronouncing for as fer, but never Rita. She didn't like any misuse of the English language, and she didn't even like colloquialisms—I wonder now if she ever knew she was using this old saying incorrectly. For almost fifty years I drifted along, ignorant, but never quite curious enough to uncover the mystery. It

Rita, age 16

was only with the desire to reflect on Dead Rita's Wisdom and begin to share it that, at last, I was brought to understand this funny little expression.

I began to think about how we communicate—how often we aren't clear. We choose to be misunderstood, or, because of our own ignorance, we don't know what we're saying. We may also choose to be clever or pithy at times, leaving our listener unsatisfied and un-fulfilled—as Rita's expression did.

And sometimes talk is just talk. I believe there are times when it's okay to not be deep or wise or terribly sincere. As a kid, I know I babbled away all the time—and I'm sure poor Rita just didn't feel like answering every question that bubbled up from me. Hence, "kit-ten britches." But I think about all the other times when she shared with me completely. She shared things that weren't always terribly important, but that brought us together. Often our conversations were easy and kind and flowed without hesitation. When you're with someone you love and you get along, that ease makes the relation-ship effortless. In this world of effort and striving and straining, our greatest rest may come from being with people we love who don't challenge us or need us to be "on." People who love us in our goof-ness and silliness. Who express their love for us both in actions and words that are simple, heartfelt, and uncomplicated.

I believe that sometimes our search for wisdom is more complicated than it needs to be. What if we stopped for a moment and simplified our feelings and emotions? Just stood in the moment. Just quieted our minds and realized that where we are is perfect. At times we may be on a big "what fer" search for the meaning of life… and in many ways the answer might be cat's fur to make kitten britches. It makes no sense, and there is no answer. It just is. Slow down and realize that it's okay to be just who you are, and you'll have rest in your quest.

Your Own Wisdom:

You and I Are One

Dead Rita's Wisdom:
If you have found oneness
with another, embrace it.

CARING FOR RITA DURING HER last months occurred in our home. It was the only way she and I wanted it to be. We had always been there for each other and so it would be through the end.

As Rita's cancer progressed, she trusted me to provide and co-ordinate all of her care. Because of the way life works out sometimes, I knew exactly what to do. With my past experience as a legal guardian, I was comfortable with the medical community, and I was familiar with everyone who could get her all the care she required. Blessedly, as a result, the process of her dying was not complicated by fear of how to access the system.

In fact, dying isn't that complicated. It's living that requires patience. Rita's secondary cancer, the lung cancer, grabbed hold of her in July 1997 and began to spread to her liver and brain. Difficult, but manageable. She was a gracious and grateful patient. What a difference that makes for caregivers, doctors, family, friends—all involved.

It's an honor to care for someone who moves beyond the anger over the injustice of death (sometimes the good do die young) and allows the journey of dying to be lived with dignity and grace.

That was Rita.

She and I wasted no time missing each other before she died.

"Mom, how can you leave me with these bozos?" I joked one day

---

When we choose to not focus on what is missing from our lives but are grateful for the abundance that's present...we experience heaven on earth.

——Sarah Breathnach

---

about a month before she passed away, referring lovingly to my two brothers and father.

She looked at me and said, "I'm so sorry, Vic." And we burst out laughing. Then, simultaneously, we burst into tears.

And so we continued walking together toward the end, her ability to participate in her care lessening and my care of her increasing. It was our journey.

She and I spoke the same language. We always had. She was my strength and I was hers.

At the end, she chose to give me another gift of her wisdom.

It was her final week, one of the days when I was the primary caregiver. I was holding her so I could turn her, and she looked up at me and said, "Vic, you and I are one."

I looked her in the eyes and said, "I know."

You and I are one. It's truly a gift to another to let them know—really know—that you love them, appreciate them, that you get them on all levels.

Rita and I didn't look alike, we spoke differently, and we believed in different things. We had different interests. We argued. We laughed. We trusted each other with our deepest thoughts. We forgave one another. We appreciated each other's strengths. We admired each other and said so. She was beautiful to me, and I to her.

We were both better for knowing each other. We shared a love for our family and we had each other when all else failed.

We were one.

We can truly say this when we become aware that another person doesn't merely complete us, but is with us in such a deeply comfortable way. In just saying, "We are one," we know it's true.

Oneness takes time. Rita knew it after forty-one years of having me in her life. The moment it was said, it was what I needed most.

Being one does not mean forever. Dead Rita is dead. She has yet to come back and visit me. I dream of her—though not so often now. And yet... we are one.

I pray that the best of Rita lives on in me. Her wisdom, kindness, creativity, love of family, her ability to celebrate others, her generosity and strength.

I've said it before: I would never trade the grief and loneliness I've known, especially in the first days after she died, for never knowing the kind of love we shared.

No regrets. No mourning for what could have been. When you are one, what was is all that counts. In that, I cannot ask for more.

If you have found that oneness with someone, express it. Share it. Embrace it. It's a rare gift.

Your Own Wisdom:

Perseverance

The Future Belongs to Those Who Believe in the Beauty of Their Dreams

Dead Rita's Wisdom:
Whatever might be stopping
you—give it up.

"*T*HE FUTURE BELONGS TO THOSE who believe in the beauty of their dreams."

Rita didn't say that. But she gave me a glass paperweight with Eleanor Roosevelt's quote on it when John and I purchased a building in 1995. The venture was a bit beyond our comfort zone, but it all penciled out and we knew it was a sound investment and part of our dream for our financial future.

Eleanor Roosevelt's words ring strong in my heart. How many times do we become so discouraged that we want to just give up on our dreams? Things don't always turn out as we hope. So little is truly in our control. And yet... and yet. The one thing we do control is our response to all that happens around us.

My behavior, my beliefs, and my attitudes are the rudder that steer my ship. The waters may often be rough. But who cares where I'm heading more than I do? Who on earth can offer me guidance if I don't turn first to my own wisdom?

Dead Rita was a great source of strength and wisdom because she loved deeply, and with others she was her best. Often she appeared to give up when it came to herself—but did she? Was she conscious of the strength and courage with which she faced the world? I like to think that she caught a glimpse, now and then.

She was a dreamer. She dreamed of being a dancer. A singer. An artist. A mother. And who knows what other dreams she never gave voice to.

She shared with me that one of her dreams was to have a little girl, a brick house, a white picket fence, and a big dog. I don't remember any picket fence. But we lived in a red brick house on Chaddsford in Fort Wayne, had a wonderful galoot of a St. Bernard, and of course there was me. When I was born with a port wine stain on my face and mouth, Rita wasn't discouraged. She somehow knew she would overcome any obstacle. That is a dreamer.

Think about what may be holding you back. About where you want to go, and what it will take. Perspective. Trust. Faith. Hope. Commit to your dream, and you'll find that each of these things will come to you. You'll never be really alone. Never without hope. Never unable to manage what lies in your path.

The future belongs to those who believe in the beauty of their dreams. I believe that is true. I've dreamed all my life of accomplishing amazing things. They may have been my own very personal quests—not blow-you-away amazing. But they've been my dreams, from early on. And I haven't been disappointed.

I dreamed of working at McDonald's the day I turned sixteen. I walked there on my sixteenth birthday in 1973 and got my first "real" job. What a thrill—and what life-changing experiences. That job taught me business lessons that I use to this day. "If you've got time to lean, you've got time to clean." Oh, I could go on!

I dreamed of going to Purdue University. Dad told me if I wanted to go to college, I could join the Army. He said, "Let them pay." I wasn't deterred—and didn't sign up for a tour of duty. I worked hard to save money. The day I stepped onto the campus of Purdue in West Lafayette, Indiana, I knew I'd reached another dream.

We're all dreamers. But consciously dreaming is different from simply letting your mind wander. Today I continue to have a lot of fantasies about things I can do, but those aren't my big dreams. My big dreams are becoming my reality. Knowing that you play a very real part in your own success can change what you believe is possible.

My passion and experience are in working with people. I worked with seniors for years. I wanted to write a book on how to do that; it's been outlined forever. But that book was never my dream. I always dreamed of dedicating my first book to Rita. Instead, I have written about her with the intention of sharing her wisdom on a bigger stage.

Dreams are so much more than the goal of the dream itself. The process with which we realize a dream—all the steps along the way—are the proof that the dream is becoming a reality, and often so much bigger than we imagined possible.

What are your dreams? Whatever might be stopping you—give it up. Give up not believing in yourself. Embody the courage you present to others. And believe, fully, in your dream. If you're a parent, a CEO, a religious leader, a teacher, a human being who believes there is more than this... you are a dreamer. And the future truly belongs to those who believe in the beauty of their dreams.

The future can belong to you.

Your Own Wisdom:

You Should Be an Accountant

Dead Rita's Wisdom:
Trust in what you want, and don't lose that trust if you don't see the whole path.

*A*T ABOUT THE AGE OF SIX, I realized that I wanted to be a nurse. I didn't know any nurses and I hadn't spent time around any of them, but their work felt glamorous and meaningful to me. And I really liked helping people. So nursing was my dream. While lots of little kids change their profession of choice with great frequency, I never wavered.

I was a voracious reader as I grew older. In the summertime, I stayed home to watch my younger brother Danny, and the library bookmobile would make its weekly stop in our neighborhood. I would check out fifteen books at a time. My favorite: the Private Duty Nurse stories, of which—oh, joy—there were many. I'd lose myself in their intrigue, glamour, romance—and the occasional murder mystery. Private Duty Nurse goes on a cruise. Private Duty Nurse takes care of the curmudgeon. Private Duty Nurse goes to Ireland to care for a heretofore unknown wealthy aunt. Nursing was the profession for me!

When I was thirteen, I became a candy striper in the local hospital. It was a strategic move on my part to ensure that I really did care for the medical milieu—and I found that I loved the energy, the work, the people. I was so enthralled that I earned my two-hundred-hour volunteer pin over that summer—in three months rather than the usual one to two years. Yessiree, I was going to be a nurse!

Mom, Loretta, me and Jeff, circa late 1950s

In high school, I took Latin so I could understand medical terminology. I took chemistry and advanced chemistry. And I had a difficult time in all three classes. I was terrible with grammar, so Latin quickly became overwhelming. Chemistry was simply awful. I believe that had I not had friends in each class, and had the chemistry teacher not liked me, I would have gone down in flames. But I persevered, determined, through my senior year.

When the time came, I enrolled in the school of nursing at Purdue University. I was going to be a nurse. I was going to reach my dream. I looked at all the science classes and hesitated: Was this what I really wanted?

While in high school, I was also involved in Junior Achievement, which taught students entrepreneurial skills and the world of business through running our own companies. For three years, I was part of a Junior Achievement company that sold "Star Lights" for eight dollars each—six glass ashtrays crackled and glued together in a decorative form. With over $3,000 in eventual sales, my partners and I had a serious little business.

At the end of our senior year, we were nominated for Junior Achievement Company of the Year. We made our way through the local and state level contests, scoring high enough to become one of the national finalists. Attending the conference with two thousand

enthusiastic, business-oriented young people was terrifically exciting.

Through the vetting of competitions, our company, Star Unlimited, placed in the top three in the nation. On stage that hot summer
night in 1975, we were named Company of the Year out of 7,000 Junior Achievement companies. As company treasurer and one of the
three representatives of Star Unlimited present at the competition,
I'd played an undeniable role in our win, and couldn't have been
more thrilled.

My role in our Junior Achievement company as the treasurer
interested me in finance. Accounting came easily to me—unlike the
sciences. I'd come to excel on a level that was exciting and interesting to me.

When I arrived home from the conference and shared the win
and my experiences with Rita, she was happy for me. We talked
about my success, and how easy it was for me to interact with pro-
fessionals, to speak extemporaneously about business, to manage
the books, to draw conclusions from numbers. She said, quite simply,
"You should be an accountant."

Rita was an accountant. Self-trained. No college—much to her
shame. But she'd found great success overseeing the books for a man
who owned multiple companies. She'd taught me how to use a ten-
key calculator as a junior in high school when I worked in the office
of a local clothing store. She knew my aptitude.

And she was right.

Her idea hit me like a bomb. I should be an accountant. Who
knew nursing would include so much science? I was drawn to the
science of healing so I could help and encourage people. But without
a moment's hesitation, I changed my intended major—feeling both
thrilled and relieved to have found the better path. I always felt as if
I'd given up on my dream of nursing.

I successfully completed my accounting degree. I became con-
troller for a manufacturing firm after I was married. And later I became a stay-at-home mom.

Eventually, when life allowed, I began doing volunteer work with
the elderly. Soon I was visiting them, balancing their checkbooks,
and providing guardianship and conservatorship services. Without
Rita's foresight and guidance, I would never have found that work or
done that job.

Becoming an accountant gave me the skills to serve the elderly

> All the knowledge I possess everyone else can acquire, but my heart is all my own.
>
> ——*Johann Wolfgang von Goethe*

on a greater scale than if I'd been a nurse. I was in and out of local hospitals to advocate with doctors, make health care decisions, and spend time with people who needed someone to care for them when they could no longer care for themselves. I eventually had a business as a fiduciary, which was large, successful, and rewarding.

I was fulfilling my dream of being a nurse by helping people. What I now understood was that, for me, being a nurse had represented the ability to care for others. Being an accountant meant managing finances so that others could be protected and cared for. In the end, my career choice was, by name, an inadequate description for how I would really live my life in service to others.

Dead Rita's simple idea became a brilliantly identifying piece of my puzzle. That training, and the background it provided me, opened up so many unforeseen opportunities in business over the years.

What we do is not who we are. But it makes perfect sense to use those skills that come naturally to us so that we can manifest our greater dreams. For me to fight through all of the challenges I'd have faced as a nursing student would have taken away my love of caring for people. I never put that dream to rest, but I was willing to do what came naturally—business. With the ease that seems to come when we follow our true passions, I circled back around to what I'd always wanted: to help others.

What comes easily for you? How can you take that strength and use it to build a bigger dream? Trust in what you want, and don't lose that trust when you don't see the whole path. You may only see the next step. Take it. Your dream lies around the next bend.

Your Own Wisdom:

This Too Shall Pass

Dead Rita's Wisdom:
It all passes, the good as well
as the bad, so stay present
with it all.

*R*ITA OFTEN DIDN'T KNOW THE answer to the challenges she and her family faced. But she always looked for some sense of hope, even when times were darkest. And isn't hope what gives us courage?

My parents filed for bankruptcy twice, once in 1975, and then again in the early 1990s when they came to live with us. Financial ruin was one of my mother's greatest embarrassments. We were quite middle-class—but it was virtually all achieved on credit. I remember how Mom would walk away when Dad would pay for something, because there was such a good chance the credit card would be denied. She was so deeply humiliated. Yet she not only stayed with my father, in many ways she enabled him to plunge the family always deeper into debt.

Somehow they survived. Had a lovely home. And when all was lost financially a second time, they came to live with John and me.

In truth it was a gift. We had over five years together—a time when Rita didn't need to worry about Dad's spending. She'd grown up extremely poor, on the wrong side of the tracks, and always felt a sense of humiliation and the very real fear of losing what she'd gained. Those five years of respite with us were a blessing.

She knew dark times in her life. She met and survived them. And when I also experienced particularly difficult times, she would

> # Life is not about waiting for storms to pass...it's about learning how to dance in the rain!
>
> *— Vivian Greene*

say, "This too shall pass."

Nothing lasts. Not greatness. Not wealth. Not difficulties. This wisdom from Rita allowed me to see that an end was in sight—to whatever I needed to see past.

I am still comforted by these words, and I have no doubt that remembering them brings solace even before I see their results.

When Mother died, I grieved. I didn't grieve while she was dying. I was too busy being with her—loving her, caring for her, not missing her before she was gone. She suffered physically and I was there through it all, not pitying her. It was simply the time to meet her needs.

I had dreams about her being gone. I would suddenly awaken and felt as if my chest was going to split open. And yet, when she did die, it was not like any dream I had dreamt. It was indescribable.

In the months following her death, I began to have terrible flashbacks. I saw again her seizures, her body carved up from cancer and surgeries, her slow decline into helplessness. Finally, I grieved. But I was afraid I was losing my mind.

I visited my favorite therapist and told her I thought I was in the midst of a breakdown. I had been so strong! So helpful! So present! And now I was so lost.

She told me I was suffering post-traumatic stress disorder—a natural result of all I had gone through in the final eighteen months of my mother's life. "What am I to do?" I asked. And she replied, "Nothing. It will fade. The memories will not be as vivid and stark. It will pass."

This too shall pass. It all passes. The good as well as the bad. We must stay present with whatever is happening. A great marriage full of love and passion can end through the death of a spouse, a divorce, an illness… it shall pass. An incredible moment of victory, accomplishment, awareness, epiphany… each shall pass. And we will still be here.

So take stock. In the darkest moments, remind yourself that "this too shall pass." It is a tender thought. It will keep you focused. It will offer strength, perspective, wisdom. And the hope to give you courage.

Your Own Wisdom:

I'm Entitled

Dead Rita's Wisdom:
You're entitled to live your
life fully and richly, exactly
as you see fit.

*T*HERE CAME A POINT IN Rita's life when she stopped believing that she didn't deserve anything. This change represented one of her most important journeys. Few things I saw in my mother's life brought me greater happiness than this self-awareness she experienced.

I frankly don't know what any of us deserve. I sometimes think I'm absolutely entitled to be struck by a lightning bolt direct from the heavens above. The law ensures us certain entitlements or rights regardless of gender, race, religion, and so on. In the extreme, a sense of entitlement is held by narcissistic individuals who simply believe the world "owes" them.

Rita certainly never suffered from that type of extreme self-entitlement. But as she grew older, evolving through the many phases of being a daughter, wife, and mother, her emotional health grew stronger. After playing each of these roles, she found something was missing: Her needs. Her desires. Her dreams.

Rita's mother never told her that she was entitled to happiness or success. In fact, her mother did her a great disservice: She raised Rita to feel a huge sense of duty to others, while feeling shame about her own needs. The shame was painful to watch. As someone who loved her dearly, I felt as if she believed she had to pay a debt she'd never incurred.

My mother's religious upbringing was spotty. My grandmother and her cousin—Madelyn Murray O'Hair, world-famous atheist—were brilliant, angry, and without a need of God. Rita, however, attended the Episcopal Church in Norwalk, Ohio, and even worked in the office. As a young adult, she attended alone. I don't even know how she found the church.

When her parents fought, she told me, she would pray that God would protect her mother. But she had no faith in herself, nor faith that God wanted her to have happiness. She married my father without truly being in love with him, then suffered humiliation through his verbal abuse during much of their forty-plus years of marriage. She sacrificed everything to raise her children the best way she could. Until near the end of her life, she never knew that she could have more.

My parents came to live with John and me in 1993, and stayed until Mother's death five years later. The move was brought on by my father's excessive spending and my mother's complacency—behaviors that had reduced their meager life savings to zero. Despite appearances, this became a ridiculously undeserved, unexpected blessing for both Rita and me!

We got to live together again. In harmony. In joy. The arrangement forced Rita to look at her life in a new way. I placed no demands on her. I only wanted her life to be as good as she had made mine. During this time, her sense of entitlement began to awaken. Once she got over the wonder of no longer fearing the future, never again to be paralyzed by my father's rage and its effect on her life, she began to feel that she deserved happiness and the freedom to be herself.

She began to paint again. To write. To use the computer for exploration and learning. To give my father (and herself) boundaries around the behavior she would accept. She was in her glory.

Then she got cancer in 1995.

She gave up. Decided not to treat it because she'd watched her beloved grandmother die a painful death from brain cancer. She believed there was no hope. When the pain was great enough and a doctor told her that a mastectomy could save her, she said, "Sure. Take it off! But," she added, "no chemo and no radiation."

Sure enough, after the surgery she kept her word, refusing either follow-up treatment. And blessedly, miraculously, the cancer had not spread to her lymph nodes—miraculous because she had waited sixteen months after her diagnosis before having the surgery.

But a year and a half later, in July 1997, the cancer returned with a vengeance. Her doctor told her that only aggressive treatment would keep her alive: chemo, lung surgery, then radiation.

This time she agreed.

What had changed? She felt entitled to live longer. She didn't want to die and was no longer a victim of circumstances. She'd realized that hers was now a richer, fuller life, and she began to fight for it.

She did it on her terms, as a trooper and a courageous woman. She would say, "I'm entitled!" And she meant it, owned it, lived it. During the last three to four years of her life, she was happier than I'd ever seen her before.

I loved watching her embrace herself as a beautiful, empowered woman. She opened her life up. She was no longer stymied and controlled by her past or by things that were not her doing, but that had been done to her.

Her wisdom served her well. It served others, by example, to an even greater extent. I often called her a martyr, but in retrospect I don't think she was. She was actually entitled to live her life exactly as she saw fit. Without the sacrifices I saw her make, so much would not have been accomplished in the world, simply by virtue of the ripples she created.

I hear her gentle voice in my mind right now saying, "Vic, I was no martyr. I lived my life the best I could. I was entitled to make mistakes. To find the better way, even if it seemed late to you. No regrets. No loss. It was my life. And it served me well."

That's just like Dead Rita. Giving me advice even as I'm writing about her advice.

The wisdom you carry within you is as great as Rita's. Tap into it and let it nourish you. Live your life, fully and richly. (Sooner rather than later is good!)

If you do it for one reason, do it because of this: You're entitled.

Your Own Wisdom:

Take Your Art to the World

Dead Rita's Wisdom:
Others often see our greatness much more clearly than we do.

*R*ITA FIERCELY LOVED MY BROTHER Jeff's children—her natural grandchildren, Joshua, Justin, and Janelle.

She was as terrific a grandmother as she was a mom. Jeff and his family lived in Indiana, and Rita loved spending time with them. After she and my Dad moved to Oregon to live with us, she'd show me cards and pictures the grandchildren had drawn and look at me very seriously and say, "These children are exceptional."

I did tease her about that. She made them sound so perfect. She loved them beyond measure and saw their deepest potential.

My own four stepchildren never had the opportunity to have that kind of relationship with her, and I resented these golden grandchildren in the Midwest even though I hardly knew them myself. In 1993, when my parents moved to Oregon, I no longer needed to go to Indiana. After they moved to Oregon I didn't return to Indiana to see my brother and his family. But Rita continued to fly there to see them whenever she managed to save the money.

Years after Mother's death, I had an opportunity to go back to Indiana for a few days. By then, my brother's children were grown: Josh was 20, Justin 18, and Janelle 13. And after all those years, they were strangers to me. Yet it soon became clear that they really were the exceptional human beings that Rita had always claimed.

During my stay, I saw a part of her in each of these young people.

Joshua, Mom, Janelle and Justin, 1997

The older two, Josh and Justin, had known Mom the best. In many discussions with all three of them, I shared how much they had been loved by their grandmother.

We talked of her kindness and love. Her creativity and generosity. And her art.

Rita was a gifted artist who could do it all: write, paint, draw, sculpt, sew, craft. Her ability was stunning, and surprised no one more than herself.

Josh had showed a talent for art early on. He'd received multiple awards in high school and was enrolled in a college arts program. His talent today is breathtaking.

One night, as he and I were talking, he told me a story. He remembered being a little boy and showing Rita his art. She had looked at him and said, "Josh, I have always hidden my talent. I don't want you to do that. Take your art to the world."

He told me from that day on he knew he would be an artist.

Josh's story amazed me. Once again, Rita's reach was beyond expectation. A simple conversation with a child had guided him toward finding his own greatness. Truly, the power of our belief in another is extraordinary.

Josh is an accomplished artist today, who credits one Rita Clark Hoering for giving him the awareness and the confidence to take his gift to the world. He's traveled to Italy to study the great artists, and his work has been displayed in museums in Indiana. There is no doubt in my mind that he is only beginning to make an impact with his art.

Rita was also a great artist. But her mother and her husband—who were most in a position to encourage her talent—were not there for her. As a result, few people ever saw the beauty that she quietly created in secret.

What "art" must you take to the world? What gifts do you keep hidden that are rarely revealed except to those you know well? And what will be lost as a result of your hesitations or insecurities?

Like George Bailey in *It's a Wonderful Life*, many of us believe we don't make a difference on this planet. If we could see the effect we have just by being, we would begin to realize that any "art" we withhold has the capacity to change life's landscape.

Some may have shared wisdom with you about your gifts. If you immediately begin to list the "why nots," pause to remember that others often see our greatness much more clearly than we can. Their greatest gift to you may be their awareness of what's possible in your life.

Listen. And take your art to the world.

Your Own Wisdom:

Step into Your Greatness

Dead Rita's Wisdom:
The result of unconditional belief in yourself gives you clarity for your own future.

I HAVE A HABIT OF EXCLAIMING in a meeting or to a client, "I have a great idea!"

The enthusiasm behind that statement is often well-founded. I don't toss it around with each and every thought I have, but I do say it when I really believe that "I have a great idea!" The confidence I express comes because my thought strikes me as one of those "where did that come from?" moments. So I celebrate my own excitement in the discovery, vocally and spontaneously, usually getting the attention of whomever I may be with, whether it's a party of one or more.

When our responses are spontaneous, pure and simple, they are often our most deeply held beliefs. Not knowing your own worth or the fact that you are capable of greatness can be the biggest barrier to your own success. My goal is always that I be the last—not the first—impediment to my success.

Dead Rita sowed the seeds for that determination.

She seemed to have no idea of her own greatness, and rarely acknowledged her wisdom or creative abilities. She was an artist of many media. She was a writer who published some articles, which made her wild with excitement and embarrassment at the same time. She was a wonderful parent. Yet she could never accept her own ability to create or develop something—even when she went

> ## What usually has the strongest psychic effect on the child is the life which the parents have not lived.
>
> — *Carl Jung*

ahead and did it despite her self-limiting beliefs. So how did she do it? How did she create? How did she see what was possible? How did she know that the answer lay right around the corner?

"It comes to me in the night," she would simply say.

That's really an "Oh, anyone could have done that" kind of attitude. Why shouldn't I acknowledge (yes, with humility but also with a certain sense of awe) that I have really brought something to the party? That what I say and believe brings value? That I'm not here on earth as a mere space holder, but have worth and value—and that every so often, I contribute something thoughtful, healing, creative, and revealing?

How often are you around others in whom you see greatness that they don't acknowledge? And if you step up and recognize their contribution or ability, are you put down for your opinion? What a waste.

I often tell clients that what stands between them and their greatness is them. No one stops you from believing in your abilities more effectively than you. Not knowing that you are blessed with certain gifts which you can tap into if you're focused enough—or not being willing to take credit for them—leads you to walk past solutions in life when you're wildly looking for an answer.

May I suggest instead that you step into your greatness—the greatness of self-awareness, not ego. Believe in what you can do. Use the gifts you've been given and encourage others to do the same. Be an inspiration not because of what you've done, but how you've done it. Be passionate and believe your dreams and goals have merit for you—and you will be inspired to tap into your deepest reserves in order to reach those personal ambitions. We're all capable. Each and every one of us.

Dead Rita and I were one. She was my "why"—the reason I am who I am today. Through example and life experience, she gave me the gift of discovering my own personal strengths and wisdoms. My own story to pass on.

Have every faith in yourself. Acknowledge your own gifts. And instead of coming to you in the night, your greatness will shine through you. Your wisdom or the wisdom you've been given by another will be fully allowed to manifest. We often walk right past the answer. We refuse to believe it's easy to be wise. In truth, reflection, remembrance and then courage to take action can manifest wisdom into your greatest moments of awareness and discovery.

Your Own Wisdom:

Epilogue

Me and mom, 1988

August 15, 1981

My dearest Vicki,

Since I can't give you a Hummel waving farewell, I thought a letter of my memories might do to start you on your new journey into another of life's experiences.

When I was five or six my dream was to have a little house with white ruffled curtains, a huge dog, and a little girl, all of my very own The years between six and twenty-three were quasi-normal, but I made it.

At 23 my dream started coming true, even though it was a little out of the sequence I had planned. Strange! First the bride in the tiny furnished apartment with the 36" kitchen, the food pantry behind the bathtub, the refrigerator in the entry hall, a bright pink dining table in the living room and an old bed with wire springs that had to be smashed against the wall every night just to stay in one spot. What a Palace! Enough of the tiny apartment experience. Besides, it wasn't even part of my dream.

How about a nice house with lots of windows for all kinds of ruffled curtains? Let me tell you about the ruffled curtains... only the young and healthy can have them. Would you believe

*washing and ironing eight pair of those suckers once a month
just because of a dumb six year old's dream? Well, believe it?
They only ruffle when they're clean. During all that washing
and ironing and toilet training a baby boy, a grand thing happened. My very own little baby girl was born. I didn't believe
it. That's pretty big stuff getting that part of a dream to come
true...it is still a marvel to me.*

*Even though the dream wasn't complete, I was much too
busy to think about it. But, alas, the dream fairy was not done
with me just yet. In fact, she was kind of a prankster fairy;
imagine, ordering my dream to be screwed up on purpose! I
forgot about the little house. Lo and behold, a brick house...
no pig could huff and puff that one down. The "little" house
was just that...TOO little. I'm talking things crammed and
stuffed into every available nook and spot. So much for "little"
houses.*

*Another baby boy, a bigger house, and guess what? The
huge dog. By this time that prankster fairy was getting a little
punchy. The huge dog was a little defective. I loved her but
after she ate all my trees, chewed on the house at snack time,
dropped elephant piles in the backyard and dug craters, I felt
like firebombing that fairy's cloud. After all the trouble I went
to keep that dog healthy and she up and died on me. I still
think eating the trees was not the best thing for her.*

*That tuckered out old fairy gave it her best shot and I love
her for all she did. The House; curtains; and dog are gone
now but old punchy created a perfect little girl for me; all the
rest of the dream was just the icing anyhow.*

*Your fairy has been busy these many years in prepara-
tion of your dreams; yours are larger than mine were. Don't
be surprised that when you least expect it one of them will
become a reality. Be prepared for the unexpected because our
fairies have a tendency to get a wee bit confused...even the
best ones. It runs in the family.*

*Now, on your wedding day, it is time for me to say fare-
well to my little girl and hello to the woman I helped create.*

*You are, and always will be, the most precious gift I was
ever given. I am giving that gift to someone else who loves
you. You are given to him, with all my love, to be treasured as
much as I have; that much love will surely protect and ensure
your happiness forever.*

"What lies behind us, and what lies before us are small matters compared to what lies within us."

— Ralph Waldo Emerson (1803 – 1882)

THERE HAVE BEEN SO MANY times when I wondered what was wrong with me. Did this relationship really exist to the depth and breadth that I felt? Was I crazy to believe that this woman loved me as purely and completely as I loved her? I felt as if I'd never know…and more than likely, I had exaggerated this love, this oneness.

In spite of my doubts and fears, I needed to share her wisdom, beauty and insight. And Dead Rita's Wisdom was born. I was afraid this was becoming a vanity project—a delusional view of a perfect relationship between two imperfect women.

And yet I wrote the words that poured out from my heart. And I smiled at the remembrances and her essence, which came through my heart and onto the paper. Though I no longer could picture her face in my mind, she lived within the memories and wisdom that I shared.

About a month ago, I found the letter, from her to me, which was dated August 15, 1981, the date of my marriage to John. And I'd never read it before! I found it in a stash of letters that I had kept, letters to me, and letters from her mother to her. I have all her papers that she saved.

I read this letter in wonderment and knew I was not mistaken. What I had remembered of her stories to me, she summed up in this simple letter. And she never sent it. I know that, because she always hand-signed all her typed letters, "all my love, Mom." This was my Mother speaking from her soul about her hopes and dreams for me in spite of her disbelief that I was marrying John.

I realized this unsent letter was a catharsis for her—and had now in a perfect way become a catharsis for me. She held me in her love from the moment I was born until I held her in my arms at the moment of her death. How simply blessed am I to have found this letter—once more giving me courage and guidance on this journey I now face without her.

My dearest Mom,

I have not wasted your hopes and dreams for my life. And because of you and your unconditional love for me, that love has protected me and ensures my happiness forever.

All my love, Vits
June 6, 2011

Bio and Contact info

Victoria Trabosh is an Executive Coach, International Speaker and Author. She has 34 years of corporate and entrepreneurial experience in manufacturing, banking, guardianships and conservatorships. She is a featured columnist for *choice*, the magazine of professional coaching, an international publication. She is also co-host of *Smart Woman Talk*, a weekly radio show (www.smart womentalkradio.com).

In addition to her coaching and speaking business, she co-founded the *Itafari Foundation*, in September 2005, a non-profit organization to change and support the country of Rwanda. Through her work with *Itafari* she had the honor of speaking at the United Nations in 2006. Victoria is passionate about changing the world with everything she does. She believes that ordinary people will accomplish the extraordinary.

Victoria lives in the Pacific Northwest with her husband, John, and two cats, Massimo and Vito. Their four grown children and seven grandchildren are never too far from their home and always in their hearts.

Victoria H. Trabosh
International Speaker & Executive Coach LLC
2187 SW Main – Suite 201
Portland, Oregon 97205
Office 503.841.6108
Fax 503.841.6092
Vicky@VictoriaTrabosh.com
www.VictoriaTrabosh.com
www.DeadRitasWisdom.com

Itafari Foundation
Victoria H. Trabosh, President and Co-Founder
www.itafari.org

Wisdom Beneath My Wings Publishing
www.WisdomBeneathMyWings.com

CPSIA information can be obtained at www.ICGtesting.com
Printed in the USA
BVOW08s1338260614

357402BV00006B/16/P